THE TEACHERS STRIKE

NEW YORK, 1968

Books by Martin Mayer

Nonfiction

The Teachers Strike: New York, 1968

All You Know Is Facts

Diploma: International Schools and University Entrance

Emory Buckner

The Lawyers

Social Studies in American Schools (*former title* Where, When
  and Why: Social Studies in American Schools)

The Schools

Madison Avenue, U.S.A.

Wall Street: Men and Money

Fiction

A Voice That Fills the House

The Experts

THE
TEACHERS
STRIKE

NEW YORK, 1968

by Martin Mayer

1817

HARPER & ROW, PUBLISHERS

NEW YORK, EVANSTON, AND LONDON

For Virginia Hardman
in memory of J. B. S. Hardman

CONTENTS

DRAMATIS PERSONAE

DR. JAMES E. ALLEN: New York State Commissioner of Education. Reluctant to involve himself or his high office in the catastrophe of the teacher strikes, he was incessantly summoned to the city by a paralyzed Board of Education and a terrified Mayor. After a number of false starts he worked out the settlement that ended the third strike.

DR. KENNETH CLARK: Professor of psychology at City University, only Negro member of the Board of Regents, and president of the Metropolitan Applied Research Center. A voice for Ocean Hill in the ear of Commissioner Allen and for practicality in the ear of Rhody McCoy, he saw his efforts tragically frustrated by a combination of bad information from his friends and brute force from his enemies.

JOHN M. DOAR: Former chief of the civil rights section of the Justice Department, now president of the Bedford-Stuyvesant Development Corporation. A newcomer to the city, innocent of its complexities, he was appointed to the Board of Education during the second teacher strike and elected its president during the third teacher strike. He opposed the settlements which ended both strikes, on the ground that

11

neither promoted voluntary compliance and a necessary peace in Ocean Hill.

DR. BERNARD DONOVAN: Superintendent of Schools. More of a politician, perhaps, than anyone else involved in this story, and much more knowledgeable about the school system, he was in the middle of every dispute, surrounded by men of principle who were not informed enough or sophisticated enough to see where their principles were leading them.

REV. MILTON GALAMISON: Minister and leader of the school boycotts of 1963–64. Appointed to the Board of Education in July, he assured its members during August that Ocean Hill was ready to settle with the union—and demonstrated his confidence in the correctness of that opinion by taking credit for the contract which settled the first strike and drove Ocean Hill to paroxysms of rage.

MAYOR JOHN V. LINDSAY: Caught in a tangle of public image, self image, naïveté and past misjudgments, he found himself playing host to a great civic disaster which acted itself out before him while he agonized over his surprising inability to control—or even to influence—the course of events.

RHODY A. McCOY: New York City schoolman of eighteen years' experience, resident of suburban Roosevelt, and unit adminstrator of the Ocean Hill–Brownsville Demonstration Project. Committed to a range of educational innovation in the project's classrooms, he made a favorable impression on all visitors. From May through December he was the only person who met regularly with all the disputants —the members of his governing board, the officers of the union and the Board of Education. Confusion followed wherever he went, as the fog follows the tide.

REV. C. HERBERT OLIVER: Minister and chairman of the governing board of the Ocean Hill project. Like Mr. Doar

12

he was a newcomer to the city, with a reputation derived from the civil rights movement: he had been part of the Southern Christian Leadership Conference. He always wanted a fight, even when others didn't; and he opposed every suggested compromise.

FATHER JOHN POWIS: Worker priest and author of revolutionary proclamations. As founder of the "People's Board of Education," which preceded the demonstration project, he became one of that body's most influential and aggressive members. The first Ford grants to the project were awarded through his church. His planned indiscretions heralded the confrontation which led to the school strikes.

MAX J. RUBIN: Lawyer, member of the State Board of Regents and former president of the Board of Education. He was sent by his fellow Regents to explore the teachers' union's real demands in the third strike, introduced Commissioner Allen to union president Albert Shanker, and ultimately invented the idea which Allen turned into a viable settlement.

ALBERT SHANKER: Former junior high school math teacher, president of the United Federation of Teachers. A product of the Socialist wing of the teachers' union, and a civil rights activist, he was goaded into violent reaction by an injustice to some of his members working in Ocean Hill and by his utter distrust of the Mayor and the Board of Education. In person and in print, he had long advocated a partnership between union teachers and Negro parents as the only hope for success in the struggle to improve urban education; now he led a series of strikes which destroyed any chance of such a partnership.

ASSEMBLYMAN SAMUEL D. WRIGHT: Lawyer and Ocean Hill resident, who represents that district and its neighbors in the state assembly. Chairman of the original planning

13

group which set up the demonstration project and member of the governing board, he broke with Rev. Oliver and McCoy over their refusal to accept arbitration of their original dispute with the teachers' union, and called for new elections for the governing board.

INTRODUCTION

The New York teachers' strike of 1968 seems to me the worst disaster my native city has experienced in my lifetime—comparable in its economic impact to an earthquake that would destroy Manhattan below Chambers Street, much worse in its social effect than a major race riot. Worst of all, the strike will very probably reduce to the condition of a Boston or an Alabama, or some mixture of the two, a school system that was wretchedly ill-organized and weakly led but relatively alert intellectually and by no means so completely ineffective as it has become fashionable to say—and that was almost the only real hope the city could offer for the future of tens of thousands of Negro and Puerto Rican children.

It is always in the interests of those in authority to say that wars and mine disasters and such are inevitable. The belief underlying this report is that what happened in New York in the fall of 1968 was *not* inevitable, and that those who are saying that it was—especially those in the great foundations, in the universities and in the Mayor's office—are much more to be blamed for what happened than are any of the partici-

15

pants. Great wealth, academic position and political leadership carry responsibilities which were not met. At no point in
the history that will be described on the succeeding pages
did these forces demonstrate any understanding of what was
happening in terms other than their own preconceptions, and
at no point did they exert the authority, leadership or even
influence which their status and social role obliged them to
exert.

As an attempt at history, the following narrative concen-
trates on events and their immediate context; and a certain
amount of background should be, as the lawyers say, stipu-
lated from the start:

1. During the course of political reform in the 1930s,
control of the New York City school system was narrowly
concentrated in a central office. In the 1950s and early 1960s
the machinery grew too complicated and too rigid for its
purposes, and the system became increasingly unresponsive
(in substance if not in public statement) to both the teachers
in the classrooms and the parents whose children were in the
schools. The teachers through trade-union organization were
able to establish countervailing force; the parents were not.
From 1961, when the state legislature mandated "revitaliza-
tion" of the local boards, which had been allowed to atrophy
since the 1930s, there has been a political drive toward
"decentralization" of the school system, to make the schools
accountable to "the community." As chairman of a local
school board, incidentally, and as a writer for various publi-
cations, I was myself among the leaders of this drive. In the
summer and fall of 1967 formal decentralization proposals
were developed by an Advisory Committee to the Mayor,
chaired by McGeorge Bundy of the Ford Foundation, for
consideration by the state legislature in the spring of 1968.
No representative of the teachers or the school supervisors,

16

the trade-union movement or the organized parent movement, was appointed to the committee.

2. In the middle 1960s the proportion of Negro and Puerto Rican children in the New York schools neared and then passed 50 percent. The proportion of Negro and Puerto Rican population in the city as a whole, however, is only about 27 percent, and the proportion of voters who are Negro or Puerto Rican is considerably less than 20 percent. New York ranks thirteenth among the nation's fifteen largest cities in the proportion of its population which is nonwhite. Within the schools the Negro and Puerto Rican children are doing substantially less well than mainland white children: at age twelve the gap between average white and average nonwhite accomplishment (excluding Orientals, who do fine) is more than two years as measured by standardized tests. It is psychologically very difficult for parents not to blame the schools; and almost equally difficult for people in the schools, who believe they are doing the best they can (and who know that their results are if anything a little better than the results in other cities), not to feel a degree of complacency in the face of failure by most of their students.

3. Most New York City schoolteachers are recruited from the city colleges, which until recently have admitted only students in the higher ranks of the city's high schools. Examinations beyond those required by the state have been imposed for a New York City teaching license, and promotion has been possible only through an elaborate system of internal examinations. Much but not all of this is mandated by state law. The proportion of Negroes and Puerto Ricans among full-time students at the city colleges has been until recently something like 3 percent; the proportion among the city's teachers is under 10 percent (by contrast with figures of 30 percent and more in other large cities, up to 80 percent in Washington, D.C.); and the proportion of Negroes and

Puerto Ricans among New York school administrators is almost invisible except at the lowest rank, that of assistant principal.

4. Ocean Hill is a border area between the slum districts of Brownsville and Bedford-Stuyvesant, some miles out from downtown Brooklyn. Less than a fifth of its adult population was born in New York City; less than a third completed high school; only two-fifths have lived in the area as long as five years; more than half the households subsist on less than $5,000 a year; about 70 percent are Negro, about 25 percent are Puerto Rican. Though there are some blocks of pleasant owner-occupied private houses, most people live in deteriorating rooming houses and tenements, and much of the area's housing is simply being abandoned by its owners. All the well-known social problems are present. It is a highly discouraging place in which to live and to bring up one's children.

THE TEACHERS STRIKE

NEW YORK, 1968

THE GOVERNING BOARD

THE POSSIBILITY OF USING the Ocean Hill–Brownsville area to demonstrate the values of community involvement in school administration was first brought to the attention of the Ford Foundation by the United Federation of Teachers. Since 1966 the union had been running a project in teacher-parent joint action—picketings and other demonstrations—which had secured the removal of an unwanted principal at J-178 (since closed as a junior high school) and had won some special services for that school and for one of the elementary schools that fed into it. The leader of these joint ventures was Mrs. Sandra Feldman, a young teacher, union field representative and civil rights worker who had been among the organizers of East River CORE, dumping garbage on the Triborough Bridge, etc. These were extremely troubled schools with limited resources, and Mrs. Feldman was in and out of them, trying to make herself useful, through 1966 and 1967.

Meanwhile, a group of social workers and parents affiliated with Brooklyn CORE and with the emerging Council Against Poverty, and led mostly by a lean and hungry worker priest,

Father John Powis of the Church of Our Lady of Presentation, had formed an unofficial "People's Board of Education" for the Ocean Hill area. Linked by their shared dislike of the Board of Education, and by their common roots in the civil rights movement, the union-sponsored marching society and the people's board joined forces in early 1967 to plan the liberation of the schools of the area from the heavy hand of the city-wide Board of Education.

It was known from the beginning that the two groups had different objectives. The people's board was interested in "community control," and the union was interested in the expansion of its More Effective Schools program, by which very substantial extra sums of money (about $600 additional per child) are invested in elementary schools to lower class size and to provide a wide range of special services. MES is extremely popular with the communities where it has been tried, however, so there was no necessary conflict between the participants in what came to be called "the planning council."

In the late spring of 1967 this planning group was recognized by the Board of Education and by the Ford Foundation, which in July put up $44,000 to pay the costs of setting up an experimental district to include the two junior high schools in the area and the five (later six) elementary schools which fed them. Any euphoria which may have been occasioned by the idea of Ford money, however, was greatly reduced at a meeting in early July with Superintendent of Schools Bernard Donovan, who informed the council that there would be no extra money whatever from the school system—and probably not much from Ford—to provide additional services for the experiment. Dr. Donovan told the group, in effect, that anybody could run better schools if he had a lot more money, and that the purpose of the experiment in community involvement was to find out whether its

22

advocates could run better schools on the same money. This statement was, of course, disappointing to all, but it made more sense to the people's board representatives than it did to the teachers.

The people's board representatives went into the summer months determined to have their project operative in the fall. They met steadily through the month of July, often with outside groups—from Ford, Brooklyn College, Yeshiva University, the Mayor's office and the Board of Education—in sessions which did not always include the teacher delegates. Among the outsiders at some of the sessions was an old friend of Father Powis', Herman Ferguson, who had recently denounced for "educational genocide" the MES school where he was employed, and who had been indicted (he was later convicted) for conspiracy to murder NAACP leader Roy Wilkins and Urban League director Whitney Young. In the absence of any systematic efforts at guidance by the Ford Foundation or the Board of Education (where the man charged with maintaining liaison with Ocean Hill took his summer vacation in July), the parent members of the planning council turned increasingly to Father Powis and to Ferguson, who was capable, forceful and extremely hostile to the union. The teacher delegates began to feel uncomfortable at meetings.

As its first step, by arrangement with Ford, the planning council hired a future unit administrator. Several candidates were interviewed by parent representatives and community leaders at sessions to which the teacher delegates were not invited, and the interviewers selected Rhody A. McCoy, a compact, thoughtful, impressive schoolman of eighteen years' experience in New York, acting principal of a school for seriously disturbed boys on the West Side of Manhattan. McCoy was also introduced by Father Powis, who had got his name from Edythe Gaines, then principal of Joan of Arc

Junior High School near McCoy's school, who knew him from district meetings and from the meetings of a new association of Negro school supervisors.

The teacher representatives on the planning council knew nothing against (or for) McCoy, but they were irked at the procedure and its speed, and a few of them thought there ought to be more than one name proposed to the full panel. Rather frivolously, on the grounds that he was somebody everyone knew, one of the teacher representatives nominated Jack Bloomfield, principal of J-271, one of the district's two junior highs. Some of the parents unquestionably felt that the teachers—authority figures in their lives at all times—were seeking to take the project away from them; and in quiet moments on Ocean Hill the reverberations of the Bloomfield nomination can still be heard. McCoy's name was quickly approved by the planning council.

Among McCoy's first acts as administrator was to authorize checks for sums of $39 to $100 for seventeen mothers of children in the district's schools, most of whom had announced that they were going to be candidates for the parent positions on whatever local board of education was set up as the result of the summer's work. These first payments were made to them as "election consultants." Some weeks after the election, in which seven of the seventeen were declared winners, the category for compensation to the lucky seven was changed to "parent representative." No public announcement was ever made that the parent representatives had been placed on the payroll, and Ford was never informed that the orginial proposal, which provided payments to board members only for attendance at training sessions, had been amended in this manner.

Payments declined as the Ford grant ran lower, rose briefly after Ford added another $15,000 in the fall, then declined again. The total up to February 1968, when the payments

opened in February. The teacher representatives felt that they did not know any of these people (except Ferguson, to whom they objected), and when they had been chosen for the planning council in June, their colleagues had never expected them to be voting on principals for the schools. The teachers announced they would abstain from the vote on the principals, and left the room during the discussion. While they did not (as some reports have had it) "bolt" the meeting—they came back after the voting on principals was finished—it is clear that their action in abstaining and leaving the room was considered a rejection of the principals by some parent and community members of the governing board.

The attempt to appoint Ferguson was gratuitously insulting to the teachers, the grand jury that had indicted him, and the city at large, but it is hard to see how the other appointments could have been avoided by any responsible board. School was to open the next week, the schools needed principals, and the Board of Education had tentatively approved the special Demonstration Principal category. Incidentally, it should be said that all but one of the principals appointed by the governing board then and later are highly regarded by both the union and by school headquarters. (The exception is Louis Fuentes, who is regarded as emotionally unstable by officials of the bureau of personnel at the Board of Education, and by the members of the local school board for District 1, whom he and his friends held physically captive for some hours one evening in September to force them to name him district superintendent.) There is an Alice in Wonderland quality about the fact that the UFT in its third strike held out for the removal of P-144 principal Ralph Rogers, who is universally admired, and of William Harris, whose sense of fairness several UFT members in the district have special reason to cherish.

The Teachers Strike the City for Their Own Reasons, and Ocean Hill Hates Them for It

Before anybody could explain to anybody else what had happened at the August 31 meeting, the teachers went out on strike against the whole city. The origins of this 1967 strike lay in a standard money dispute with the Board of Education, but its proximate cause was technical—to force Mayor John V. Lindsay to bargain with the union. The Mayor had used the teacher negotiations to try out a new technique for labor-management relations in public service—a fact-finding board which would bring in a recommendation that the Mayor would publicly announce and then impose equally upon the department of government involved and the union representing its employees. This approach, whatever its virtues, was defective in that it left the union no function. If all goodies were to come by award from the Mayor's panels, and the decisions of these panels were to be beyond negotiation, then why should public employees pay dues to a union, which couldn't do anything for them anyway? The award the fact-finders had brought to Gracie Mansion was extremely generous, and the union could not seriously have fought for more money without looking greedy. To bring Mayor Lindsay to the bargaining table, then, the union proclaimed a strike mostly for smaller class sizes, additional MES schools, etc.: "TEACHERS WANT WHAT CHILDREN NEED."

Ocean Hill parents thought that what children needed was an open school and (those who knew about it) a shiny new governing board; and the strike was an abomination. (Some also resented a union demand that teachers have the right to exclude "disruptive children" from their classrooms without waiting for the principal to decide how much trouble such an action might cause him; this issue could be, and was, presented as racist, and in part, no doubt, it is—but the question is not simple.) The union asked the governing board to support the strike and keep the schools closed. There is some dispute as to whether or not the union offered a *quid pro quo* in terms of subsequent political support of the project—Rev. Oliver has said that it did, and union president Albert Shanker has said that it did not, that support for the strike was claimed on the basis of the planning council's agreement in the spring to push for More Effective Schools. In any event, the governing board angrily refused.

In retrospect, it seems obvious—indeed, it seemed obvious at the time—that, whatever the merits of the city-wide strike, a decent sensitivity to the newly aroused hopes of the people in the three demonstration districts should have permitted the union teachers to stay on the job in Ocean Hill.

Nowhere in the city were more ardent efforts made to keep the schools open through the strike. Letters were sent from Ocean Hill to the draft boards of male teachers, announcing that the teachers were no longer teaching and should be called up. Traveling militants were brought into the schools to take classes and to scare the teachers on the picket lines. (Ferguson himself ran the training lessons for parents who were going to take over classrooms.) Curses and obscenities were screamed at the pickets from all directions, and some were jostled. When the strike ended, after two wretched weeks, many union teachers did not wish to return to Ocean Hill at all. A special meeting was held in a ballroom of the Americana Hotel, where Shanker and Sandra Feldman, who had continued to hold the union's brief on Ocean Hill, urged the teachers to go back to their schools and give the demonstration project a chance.

The union's other gestures in the weeks after the strike, however, were determinedly hostile. Because the new governing boards were beginning to claim the right to fire

31

teachers, and certainly to evaluate their performance, the UFT executive board voted to forbid union teachers to become members of such boards. And meanwhile the union joined with the Council of Supervisory Associations, the organization of the principals, assistant principals, bureau chiefs, etc., in their lawsuit to oust the new Ocean Hill principals as illegally appointed.

The impact of this lawsuit within the schools was greater than most commentators have realized. Three of the four new principals appointed that fall were beginners at their jobs, and inevitably insecure. This statement that the assistant principals and teachers did not regard the principals as legitimate or permanent damaged their ability to control what were at best difficult schools. It was easy to believe that anything unpleasant which happened in school had been organized by a subversive staff; and in some instances, probably, the belief was true. The district's teachers were placed in an almost equally difficult position, of course, in their relations with the principals. The UFT had not consulted the teachers in the district before joining in the CSA suit. Recently, Albert Shanker was asked why the union had taken this action, especially in the light of its long history of opposition to the principals' licensing exams (the union has always advocated the election of principals by teachers). Shanker said, "Pure pique."

In November the administrative structure of the Ocean Hill schools collapsed: eighteen assistant principals applied for transfer out. New APs (assistant principals) were transferred in from the Board of Education list; the right to nominate principals without city license was all the special authority over personnel the Board planned to give to Ocean Hill. The governing board would plead unheard a few months later that "The very best principal in the world cannot operate a school with assistant principals who are not cooperating."

Frustration Overwhelms the District and Radicalizes Its Governing Board

Meanwhile, McCoy was having serious difficulties setting up his own office. His application for a telephone was delayed from mid-July to September 6, and until space in a new apartment house became available around the first of the year the Board could find no better headquarters for him than an unheated store front. McCoy was denied the privilege of giving his appointees instant tenure, which meant that people transferring into Ocean Hill from out-of-town schools were risking their future livelihoods. Two assistants who lacked New York City licenses were denied formal appointment for some months, though McCoy was able to pay them on the school system's lower per-diem consultant rate. (Ford grant money could not be used to pay people in operating positions.)

The Board of Education denied requests for lump-sum budget allocations for McCoy's office and for the schools, insisting, for example, that money allocated from the central office for library would have to be spent for books and could not be spent for teacher training. Partly to employ local people and partly to get some authority over spending, the governing board asked for the right to let its own contracts for maintenance of its mostly decrepit school buildings, and was refused. Some of these powers the Board of Education probably could not have delegated legally, and some (considering what was being done with the Ford money) it was probably wise to refuse. But Board member Lloyd Garrison, for one, thought that insufficient effort was put into searching the statutes to see what, if anything, could be done to increase the authority of the demonstration district governing boards.

The new semester in February 1968 brought fresh problems and promises. The new I-55 was opened with gleeful ceremony, and the old J-178 was converted to an elementary school, ending overcrowding in the district. Ferguson was still unacceptable to the Board of Education, and the governing board appointed Percy Jenkins acting principal of I-55. An experienced principal of Chinese background, Daniel Lee, was brought in from Nassau County for the converted P-178, and a principal of Italian origin was appointed to P-73. Jack Bloomfield of J-271, whose relations in the district had disintegrated after his nomination to be unit administrator, had finally been granted his transfer out. McCoy wanted to shift William Harris to J-271 from the now defunct J-178 because J-271 was his worst problem and he considered Harris his best man (so did the J-178 teachers, nearly all of whom signed a petition asking the governing board to allow Harris to move with them to I-55). The Board of Education would not make the appointment, however, and finally McCoy in desperation simply "recognized" Harris as principal of J-271. (The Board had a reason for its reluctance, by the way—Allen had authorized *elementary* school, not junior high school, demonstration principals.) Now only one pre-governing board principal was left in the district.

Harris, the first male Negro principal of a secondary school in New York, came into an unbelievably chaotic situation. Thirty teachers—a quarter of the staff—had transferred out, and the Board of Education had found only sixteen replacements. Five of the six secretaries had left; all the assistant principals were new; and forty sets of keys were missing. Absenteeism ran from ten to twenty-five teachers a day; often there were simply not enough adult bodies in the building to man the classrooms for seventeen hundred children, let alone

34

to chase the kids out of the halls. Fires broke out mysteriously, several every week, and the culprits could not be found. Furniture was thrown from third-floor windows, paint flew around art rooms, vandalism and thievery were everywhere. Harris met grimly with his staff, and they decided they would try to make it work. Somehow.

In early March, Justice Dominic S. Rinaldi of Kings County Supreme Court handed down an opinion that the appointment of Demonstration Elementary School Principals in Ocean Hill was illegal under Subdivision 10 of Section 2573 of the Education Law. The next day Frederick Nauman, a guidance teacher who was UFT chapter chairman for J-271 and district chairman for the unit, drafted a letter to Alfred A. Giardino, president of the Board of Education, urging him to appeal the decision and to retain the governing board's principals on the job pending the results of the last possible appeal, because the Ocean Hill experiment was important and would be killed if the principals were removed. Nauman secured 115 signatures, virtually the entire staff, and sent the letter off. Giardino received and acknowledged it with the comment that the Board was proceeding along the lines Nauman and the J-271 staff desired.

When I arrived at Ocean Hill that month to write an article, I found McCoy working desperately hard with his principals and staff—some white, some Negro—to put a head of steam under a number of new programs in reading, math, Negro and Puerto Rican culture, bilingualism, etc. He had begun small-scale training programs for "paraprofessionals," mothers of children in the district's schools who would at the end of the programs become teacher assistants, helping out with reading and math. He was planning for teacher teams, nongraded classrooms, programed instruction—everything in the way of educational innovation that might help in a neighborhood where most children were as far behind as they were in Ocean Hill. I visited four of the district's schools on as many days, and returned to tell McCoy that I had seen a good deal of routine and some substandard teaching, and that the schools seemed dominated by a fear of disorder which impeded teaching. He said he knew, that he was working to establish a climate in which teachers could teach, and that once he had the climate he was going to judge who was good and could give help, who needed help, and who ought to be eliminated from the district. It was all intelligent, level-headed and very sad.

During April, 1968, the district sustained three serious shocks. One was the murder of Martin Luther King and consequent assaults on white teachers at J-271, some of which may have been stimulated by an inflammatory notice about the assassination posted on bulletin boards by Leslie Campbell, publicity director of the African-American Teachers Association, who had recently transferred into the district. Another was a two-day school boycott called by the governing board and almost entirely effective, to support the governing board's demand for recognition and for authority over budget and personnel. The third was a fire one afternoon at I-55, which drove everyone out of the building a little after two o'clock. At three the firemen were still there, and the children were still on the street. A few teachers—there is a dispute about how many, but ten would seem to be a maximum figure—simply abandoned their classes and went off home, or to their second jobs, or whatever. When the children poured back into the building, coats and other possessions were stolen, fights broke out, and the new school, which had opened three months before as the future pride of the community, became the scene of a minor riot.

At about this time, perhaps because of the general level of frustration, perhaps because of these specific events, perhaps because the Ford grant had run out and the parent representatives were no longer being paid—perhaps because it had been planned that way from the beginning—the Ocean Hill board fell under the domination of people who had determined to use it to "force a confrontation with a sick society."

PART II

THE CONFRONTATION

COMPLAINTS AGAINST TEACHERS are endemic to the process of education. Most often they are ill-founded, the result of childish incomprehension or parental disappointment, and to protect teachers against such complaints and against politically motivated discharge, rules of teacher tenure have been adopted throughout the civilized world. Teachers can still be removed for malfeasance, but in most school systems it is bloody difficult—in New York just the nuisance of written charges and hearings and appeals makes any administrator blanch at the notion of actually seeking to dismiss anyone. In fact, only twelve teachers have been formally discharged, from a teaching force of more than 57,000, in the last five years. Sometimes a teacher can be persuaded to resign under threat of disciplinary action. Usually, though, a supervisor with an intolerable teacher rids himself of the offending atom by arranging a voluntary transfer. One of the survival skills of a New York school administrator is the ability to slough off bad staff onto other districts, and there are literally hundreds of incompetent (some of them mentally ill) teachers drifting about the school system.

Inevitably, Ocean Hill got more than its share of bad teachers. After Mrs. Feldman and Shanker had persuaded the striking teachers to return to the demonstration unit in fall 1967, the UFT got to work on escape hatches for them in case the situation turned nasty. As part of an effort to keep teachers in slum schools, the Board of Education and the union some years before had worked out a contract provision that teachers could not apply for transfer until they had five years' seniority, and that no more than 5 percent of the staff of any school would be permitted to transfer during a school year. When the demonstration projects were announced in spring 1967, the union had staked out a position that these projects would be outside the contractual limitation on transfer, that participation in them would be voluntary. After the 1967 strike the union began meeting with the Board of Education to iron out transfer rules for Ocean Hill and for the IS-201 complex in East Harlem, where the teachers were even more frightened. Obviously, mass transfer out would kill the projects, leaving a huge reservoir of ill will in the neighborhoods. The union agreed to (Shanker says it proposed) a compromise, by which 10 percent of the staff could transfer out of a demonstration district at the end of each semester—20 percent a year. Ocean Hill was never consulted about these arrangements (a true case of colonialism), and deeply resented them. In the event, the contract did no good—nearly 20 percent of the teachers left Ocean Hill when the term broke February 1. The bureau of personnel could not replace them all, and some of the replacements it did find were pretty bad.

Ocean Hill administrators were getting complaints about good teachers, too, because, after all, what's the use of having a home-grown governing board if they can't do anything about the teachers? McCoy and his staff had little time

40

to sort out complaints, which was resented, as it always is. (Slums and suburbs are more alike than most commentators think, because people live in both.) Receiving what they considered short shrift from the professionals, some Ocean Hill parents went to their friends on the governing board, to the point where on February 28 the by-laws of the governing board were amended to state that the board would not hear complaints brought by its members against professional personnel.

McCoy, meanwhile, was disturbed about the attitudes of some of the assistant principals, as reported back to him by the principals. Superintendent Donovan transferred out five APs for him on administrative request, but he reported to the governing board that requests to transfer three others had been refused. He may have meant only that he had been told those five were his full quota, because no specific request to move out an AP was ever denied. The governing board met to discuss the reported refusals, and someone suggested that the board should simply exclude the APs from the district. On March 28 this tactic was rejected, mostly on the urging of Assemblyman Wright, who thought there was a chance to get an effective school decentralization bill through the legislature, and felt that any arbitrary action by the governing board would harm its chances. He proposed that the board announce charges against the APs and hold public hearings before taking any action, and his motion carried. The next day Wright went back to Albany, the governing board met again, and the motion passed the previous day was rescinded. At these meetings board members began discussing the possibility of excluding from the district some of the teachers as well as the assistant principals. It occurred to someone that the governing board could make a very big splash in the world by firing a bunch of teachers and adminis-

41

trators and proclaiming that now and forevermore Ocean Hill would make its own decisions about who could and who could not teach in its schools.

The Governing Board Dismisses the Wrong Teachers for the Wrong Reasons

Setting up a confrontation by dismissing teachers was more difficult than the casual observer might think, because Donovan was ready to help McCoy quietly transfer out people he didn't want, and had indeed offered to do so. Involuntary transfers are not uncommon in the school system, because the procedure is useful in avoiding discharges and because something of the sort is necessary to staff new buildings with experienced teachers. When McCoy mentioned to Donovan that some people were going to have to go, Donovan told him to send along the names with some notion of the reasons why, all in confidence, and the bureau of personnel would take care of the matter.

The union, too, was ready to help out. McCoy early in the year had moved to restore good relations with the UFT. He went to Manhattan and met at union headquarters with Shanker and Mrs. Feldman and others, to ask what technical assistance the union could give him. A committee was set up, consisting of the chapter chairmen at the schools in the district plus the teacher members of the summer's planning group, and as its first order of work the committee began preparing a proposal by which P-144 in the district could be made more like a More Effective School without substantial additional expenditures. Liaison between the committee and McCoy was provided by Mrs. Feldman, who went to his office several times a month. McCoy complained that the ideas coming out of the union committee were not very good, and Shanker proposed a summer conference, an "Arden

42

House meeting," to which the union could bring its full consultative resources. At several meetings in March, McCoy mentioned to Mrs. Feldman that he was under pressure to get rid of some teachers, and Mrs. Feldman said that if he gave the UFT the reasons why he wanted to remove any individual, the union would make no trouble. To say the least, it did not occur to Mrs. Feldman that four members of the committee formed to help McCoy were among those tagged for removal.

At no time did McCoy mention to his governing board any of his renewed contacts with the union. It is interesting to note that relations between the governing board and the union teachers were so remote that no word of these meetings between McCoy and the UFT filtered through to the board members, who learned about them for the first time when Shanker mentioned them on a television show during the strike—at which point the ladies of the governing board got hopping-mad.

Some time in early March Rev. Oliver appointed a personnel committee of the governing board, with Father Powis as its chairman (though Mrs. Clara Marshall later signed its report). Some time in early April the report of the committee was ready. It recommended "the removal from our district" of the one surviving preproject principal, five assistant principals and thirteen teachers. Now came the tricky part. If McCoy had asked Donovan to transfer these people out, most of the confrontation would have been lost. (Considering the names on the list, McCoy would not have been granted all he asked for, but he would certainly have gotten most. John H. Niemeyer of Bank Street has pointed out that during this period the IS-201 complex quietly transferred out, by informal administrative procedure, more people than Ocean Hill tried to move.) At the same time, the parent representatives, and community representatives like Assem-

43

blyman Wright and Professor Stephen Lockwood of Brooklyn College (who had been co-opted as the university member of the governing board), had to be convinced that McCoy had asked for the transfers and had been refused.

And the trick was accomplished. To this day, most members of the governing board believe that McCoy asked to be relieved of the people whose names were mentioned in the personnel committee report, and got nowhere. Most outside observers think so, too, either because McCoy told them so (as he did Kenneth Clark) or because it stands to reason. In his ruling on the charges finally brought against ten of the teachers by McCoy, Judge Francis E. Rivers noted in passing that "if the Unit Administrator had sent to the Superintendent of Schools a simple request to transfer the teachers, without assigning any supporting charges, he (the Superintendent) may have been able to do so without a hearing." In its statement of opinion *The Burden of Blame,* the New York Civil Liberties Union comments in outrage, "Which is, of course, precisely what McCoy had done." But the NYCLU does not seek to explain why Judge Rivers would so clearly imply that McCoy had *not* done so if in fact he had.

The statement that McCoy never asked Donovan to transfer out any teachers does not rest on a belief that Bernard Donovan's word is necessarily better than McCoy's. In fact, McCoy has admitted to several university and foundation advisers to the project—and to me—that he never made such requests for transfer. (He says it would have been pointless, because Donovan would have refused them.) He could scarcely claim otherwise to anyone who had been nosing around the situation. There are no documents to support a claim that requests were made ("Where are his carbons?" Donovan asked sourly when told McCoy had said he asked for transfers). There is the fact that in several of the cases which reached him Judge Rivers ruled that the charges

44

against the teacher could not stand because nobody had ever notified him of his errors prior to the governing board's action in dismissing him—but surely a request for involuntary transfer would have been brought to the teacher's attention, and such indications of dissatisfaction would have constituted notice.

Despite his apparent cooperation in preparing the confrontation, McCoy seems to have avoided identifying himself with the specific action of the governing board. About a week before the dismissals occurred, Father Powis told a meeting of the Coordinating Committee for Community Control that Ocean Hill was about to "fire" thirteen teachers, and that McCoy opposed the idea. Certainly McCoy had nothing to do with the personnel committee report and recommendations which the governing board approved. Two of the teachers whose dismissal was recommended by the committee were identified only as "Mr. Steinberg" and "Mr. Bergen," and however inefficient an administrator may be he would at least know the first names of the teachers he was seeking to discipline.

In late April, just before the governing board acted, some trial balloons were lofted to see how people favorably inclined to the experiment would react to an attempt to oust teachers. One such balloon, indeed, came in my direction, when Father Powis called to inform me, rather excitedly, of the abandonment of pupils following the I-55 fire, and to say that something was going to have to be done to get those teachers "and some of the old-line UFTers who are sabotaging the project" out of Ocean Hill. It sounded to me like rhetoric, and I probably grunted assent. (I also called principal Percy Jenkins at I-55 to try to get the story straight: he was most distressed that anybody was spreading the story, played it down and defended his teachers.)

A far more important sampling of reactions occurred on

45

April 26, when members of the governing board met with members of the Urban Coalition education task force at the offices of the Carnegie Corporation. Most of the meeting was devoted to a discussion of the governing board's grievances against the Board of Education. Then, as people were putting on their coats, Father Powis announced, "Next Monday, we're firing thirteen teachers"; and everybody sat down again for a while, and listened to Father Powis' tale of the I-55 fire and unspecified "sabotage" by union teachers. John Simon, president of the Taconic Foundation and a lawyer, says that he urged Father Powis to prepare charges against anybody the governing board wished to dismiss; and Father Powis said, "No—every time you bring charges, you lose." Simon recalls asking consultant Preston Wilcox to go out to Ocean Hill and persuade the governing board to cool it, at least for the period when the legislature would be considering school decentralization proposals, but the matter cannot have loomed large, for Wilcox does not recall such a mission.

In fairness, there is a limit to how censorious I can be about the failure of the Urban Coalition to react more strongly at the time to Father Powis' announcement, for even after the event I continued to be sympathetic myself to what I thought the governing board had done. I spoke to McCoy on the telephone the day the news became public. "I want the record to show," he said, "that this community behaved very well under severe provocation for eight months. There are no charges against most of these people—they're just hostile, it's something you *sense*. But they're going to make me bring charges, and they're going to try to make the community take them back."

Not listening very carefully, my mind full of Father Powis' stories about the I-55 fire, my heart in the highlands, I said, "How big an army are they going to bring with them to make the community take them back? . . ."

46

Then it developed, astonishingly, that the teachers against whom the governing board was acting were not the I-55 teachers who left after the fire, and some were not even among the incompetents whom any visitor to the district might have noted. Two were UFT chapter chairmen, two others were original participants in the planning council, and the majority were from J-271, which was still short of staff and needed everybody it could get. Of the six J-271 teachers on the list (the committee report showed seven, but one had recently transferred into an elementary school, which the committee didn't know), principal William Harris was willing to certify that two were in fact incompetent, but against the other four he had no complaint whatever. The committee assured him that the charges against those four had nothing to do with competence, that the members of the committee had been around Ocean Hill longer than Harris and had reason to know these four were bad men and enemies of the project. The leading figure among the four was Fred Nauman, the UFT chapter chairman, who had organized the letter urging the retention of the Ocean Hill principals while the decision against their legality was appealed.

The fact is that the objection to Nauman was simply a generalized rumor of hostility which had been deliberately fed to a few parents. When the time came to present evidence against Nauman before Judge Rivers, the governing board could produce none. Mrs. Clara Marshall of the governing board said the other day, "Nauman had been beautiful, one of the best teachers in the school. But after Mr. Harris came in he *changed*. The parents said all those awful things were happening and Nauman knew about them, so he must have had something to do with them. . . ." But Nauman has letters of commendation and thanks from Harris for his work in those first weeks of the new regime at J-271, and to this day neither man has been willing to say a word against the other. Nauman rubbed McCoy wrong, but at bottom he was being discharged from the district for one reason alone: because he was the UFT district chairman. The union would *have* to fight on his behalf. Nauman's presence on the list guaranteed the confrontation. "Nauman and the others are straight arrows," Shanker said the other day in the courtroom where he was being tried for violation of the Taylor Law, "and that made it easier for us. I probably would have fought anyway, but this way my conscience is clear."

In the months since, a number of supporters of the governing board, especially the New York Civil Liberties Union, have insisted that what the board was doing was simply a routine transfer-out which the union blew up to vast proportions as part of its war against decentralization in the state legislature. There is absolutely no evidence to support this contention in the documents of the time. The report of the personnel committee, after listing the teachers to be removed, continues: "We feel that we will be condemned by many as having to make this unpleasant recommendation." In conversations at the time, Father Powis and others spoke of "firing," and in statements to the newspapers the governing board spoke of "ousting."

The letter approved by the governing board to be sent to the dismissed personnel read, in its entirety:

The Governing Board of the Ocean Hill–Brownsville School District has voted to end your employment in the schools of this district. This action was taken on the recommendation of the Personnel Committee. The termination of employment is to take effect immediately. In the event you wish to question this action, the Governing Board will receive you on Friday, May 10th at 6 P.M. at I-55.

Of course, the governing board could not fire anybody: it didn't employ anybody. Its own headquarters staff were all officially employed by the Board of Education. But it is hard to think of any accusation more likely to damage the future career of an urban teacher than a statement that he is hostile to the legitimate aspirations of Negro parents and children, and is thereby "causing serious danger to our students." That accusation was made against Fred Nauman and at least three others, officially, publicly, without evidence, after an investigation so trivial that it failed to turn up the first names of two of the persons accused. Such behavior by a public body can be defended, perhaps, by those who believed in the 1950s that the federal government was right in publicly labeling people "security risks," without evidence and falsely, and transferring them to "nonsensitive" jobs. People who opposed McCarthyism in the 1950s, though, would not seem to have available to them today the luxury of supporting the action the Ocean Hill governing board took on May 7, 1968.

Over the weekend before, Assemblyman Wright had pleaded with the governing board not to take arbitrary action on personnel the week the state legislature was to begin its consideration of decentralization bills. Nevertheless, when the governing board met that Tuesday evening in executive session, the report of the personnel committee was called up for approval. Professor Lockwood opposed the report, and urged that the board at least call the accused staff before it to talk over charges before acting. Especially when complaints relate to behavior rather than to competence, he argued, people must be given a right to some kind of hearing. Moreover, if the teachers refused to appear at the meeting, they would hand the governing board evidence to support a charge of insubordination.

Several of the parent members stirred uneasily while Dr. Lockwood spoke, and Rev. Oliver moved to the attack. The Board of Education, he said, had never recognized the governing board, which was thus not legal, and could not

49

maintain charges of insubordination against teachers who refused to appear before it. Presently, as though on signal, the door to the meeting room burst open and fifteen to twenty militants rushed in and ranged themselves against the wall. This was a community board, they said, and they were the community, and they were there to see that the board did what the community wanted. ("At this point," the minutes of the meeting say gallantly and rather glumly, "the community entered the room.") In this atmosphere the report of the personnel committee was approved, and McCoy was ordered to write letters to the nineteen, "terminating their services" in the district.

On the poisoned ground of educational failure on Ocean Hill, the governing board had sown the dragon's teeth of personal injustice. And the armed men sprang up.

The Union Strikes the Project

The next weeks saw a succession of premieres of events that were destined to have long runs. Teachers were blocked trying to enter school, police escorted teachers into buildings, parents boycotted schools, residents of the area were arrested, lights burned until three in the morning at Gracie Mansion while Mayor Lindsay met with members of the Board of Education (on the night of May 14; the issue, believe it or not, was whether it would be the Board of Education or the Mayor who issued the order to the police to escort the teachers).

Both the governing board and the union began what would be a dreary round of clevernesses. McCoy would admit the dismissed teachers to their classes, then order them to his office, and when they did not come, he dismissed them anew for insubordination. The union would arrange to have its other members wait outside the schools for the appearance of the dismissed teachers, and when their entrance was blocked, the others would all declare themselves locked out. About 350 of the district's 500-odd teachers supported the strike.

The UFT took the position that however one defined the action of the governing board it was certainly punitive, and that teachers could not be punished except on charges backed by evidence. The Board of Education agreed, and on May 14 appointed Judge Francis E. Rivers, who had recently retired from civil court after a long career as one of the city's few Negro judges, to be the trial examiner on whatever charges McCoy might bring. The governing board responded by calling for mediation by state authorities, which Superintendent Donovan accepted; but when McCoy turned up to meet with the mediators, it turned out that what the governing board meant was mediation of its claim to authority to exclude anybody without giving reasons, not mediation of the cases of the individual teachers and administrators.

Donovan brought McCoy and Shanker together, and McCoy assured both men that there were charges aplenty against the six administrators and twelve teachers (the thirteenth, the one Negro, had been reinstated almost immediately by the governing board). Not all the charges, though, were going to be publishable. For example, one of the men at J-271, a man with a family, was shacked up with one of the girls across the street, which was damaging to the morale of the school. McCoy couldn't put that in the public charges (indeed not, Donovan murmured), but if the matter came to a hearing, it would have to come out, which would ruin the man's life. Shanker agreed that was a problem, and spoke with the teacher McCoy had accused, who roared with laughter and said there was nothing to it and he would happily take his chances at a hearing. In the end, Shanker

51

continued his demand that McCoy state the governing board's reasons for compelling the transfers, and permit the accused teachers to require the presentation of evidence at a hearing. And McCoy insisted that the community had the right to decide who would and who would not teach in its schools, and that the governing board had forbidden him to present formal charges.

Meanwhile, Donovan was under pressure from Mayor Lindsay (who spoke to him directly almost daily) to get the Ocean Hill staff to accept their removal from the project. He succeeded with the administrators, all of whom eventually accepted reassignment elsewhere, but ten of the teachers were made of stronger stuff—and their union was striking to support them.

In Albany the UFT was riding the gift horse from Ocean Hill to trample the strong decentralization legislation recommended by Mayor Lindsay and by the Board of Regents. The Urban Coalition, the Ford Foundation and even the Mayor's office put pressure on the governing board to prefer charges against the teachers and to present evidence before Judge Rivers. McCoy went to Dr. Kenneth Clark, state Regent and professor of psychology at City University, and asked him to persuade the State Commissioner of Education to intervene. He assured Clark that he had gone through all normal procedures seeking the removal of the teachers, and that the governing board had finally acted the way it had because all legitimate avenues had been blocked. It never occurred to Clark that McCoy was not telling him the truth. It never occurred to the Urban Coalition groups or to the Mayor's office, until some time in November, that in fact there never had been any charges against several of the dismissed teachers. Some of the crusaders, of course, never cared whether there were any real charges against the teachers.

On May 25 Donovan put McCoy under orders: either he

would mandate on his principals the return of the teachers or he would be fired himself for insubordination. On that pledge, Shanker urged his teachers to return, and they did. McCoy promptly suspended six of them on formal charges submitted to headquarters. Donovan ordered the teachers to report to headquarters, and the union struck again. By then the state legislature had passed the Marchi Bill on decentralization, a weaker though (as the summer would demonstrate) potentially significant measure supported by the union; and the strike could no longer be considered by anyone as a political gesture to affect what happened in Albany. The union was going to see to it that the teachers kept their jobs.

The Board of Education and Ted Kheel Try to Settle the Strike Against the District

The filing of charges made this situation look like a relatively familiar kind of dispute, and the Board of Education was now confident it could be resolved in relatively familiar ways. All parties were summoned to a meeting at the Board on Friday, May 31. (That morning Rivers began hearing the charges McCoy had brought.) The Board had met twice with the whole governing board in February and April, and felt that such overpopulated conferences were no use for reaching agreements, so the instructions to Ocean Hill were to send no more than three people. The idea of delegating authority—particularly in relations with the outside world—has never been accepted in the governing board, and these instructions aroused hostility to the forthcoming meeting. The Ocean Hill delegation consisted of Vice Chairman Mrs. Clara Marshall, Father Powis and McCoy. Mrs. Rose Shapiro, acting president of the Board of Education, opened the meeting with a statement that nobody was going to leave the building until a settlement had been reached.

And, apparently, a settlement was reached. If the governing board did not wish to go through the usual Board of Education trial examiner's procedure, Mrs. Shapiro suggested, outside arbitration could be invoked and made binding on all parties. The American Arbitration Association had been set up to move expeditiously on just this sort of case. An arbitrator acceptable to both sides could be assigned on Monday, June 3, evidence could be presented to him through the week, and he could hand down his decision on Friday. Meanwhile, the teachers would go back to work, except for those dismissed by the district, who would be needed at the arbitration hearings anyway.

A one-page agreement was drawn up and typed, by which Mrs. Marshall and the Board of Education and the union all agreed to arbitration. Just before it was to be signed, Father Powis objected that Mrs. Marshall could not bind the governing board, and that the language should be changed. The document actually signed, therefore, includes a penciled insertion of the word "consider" before the word "arbitration." Nevertheless, the Board of Education and the UFT left the May 31 meeting with the feeling that the fight was over. Mrs. Marshall made an optimistic statement to the television cameras.

That Sunday Mrs. Shapiro received a call at her Westport house, from David Seeley, Mayor Lindsay's educational liaison man. Seeley said that Mrs. Marshall wanted to speak with her. Mrs. Marshall did speak with Mrs. Shapiro, and told her that the governing board had indeed considered arbitration, and had rejected it. The strike against the district went on.

Through Clark, the Ocean Hill governing board now appealed to Commissioner Allen to intervene personally. Allen replied that he couldn't, because as chief state school officer he had to remain available for any possible appeal process. (The union probably would have rejected Allen anyway, because of his close identification with the decentralization plan Shanker had fought.) Allen recommended Theodore Kheel, the city's best-established and most famous labor mediator, who is also chairman of the board of Clark's Metropolitan Applied Research Center.

A meeting was set up by Clark for Kheel's law office in midtown Manhattan at two-thirty on Friday afternoon, June 7. At two-thirty delegations from the Board of Education and from the UFT appeared at Kheel's office, but the governing board did not. Kheel called Clark, who apologized, said he would find out, then called back and said something unspecified had gone wrong and the governing board would be there at five. In fact, the governing board showed up, about a dozen strong, at seven-thirty in the evening.

The meeting in Kheel's offices lasted several hours, and, again, appeared to be productive. Kheel's position was that all parties should look to the future more than to the past. There was a need to establish fair procedures for involuntary transfer. There was assistance the union could give the governing board, especially in hiring for next fall. And there was the special problem of the dismissed teachers, and of the 350 or so who had struck. With reference to the individual cases, Kheel would look into the charges and make recommendations (not binding in form, but understood to be so in substance). This would take a while, especially as Kheel himself was due in London for a meeting on how to settle labor disputes, and would have to leave that weekend. Two of his associates—one white, one Negro—would meanwhile look into the situation.

As to what would happen in the interim, Kheel would follow the labor arbitrator's standard procedure. His aides would look at the charges against the individuals. Where the charges seemed serious on their face, they would order that the teachers be kept off the job pending a resolution of the matter. Where the charges seemed relatively minor, they would order the teachers on the job pending resolution. Both the governing board and the union were given to understand that a bare majority would be kept out of the district, while a minority would be returned, at least for the time being.

All this Kheel developed in a five-point proposal, of which point four was payment for the teachers who had struck or been locked out, depending on your point of view, for the last four weeks. The UFT accepted the proposals, though Shanker was concerned about the loss of city-wide uniformity in disciplinary procedures, disliked the inclusion in the proposal of those who had not yet been charged with anything, and was less than happy about the apparent sacrifice of six or seven of his people.

The union, the Board of Education, Kheel and Clark all say that the dispute came closer to a solution at this moment than it ever did before or since. In fact, it came closer than they knew. On Monday, June 10, the governing board met and Assemblyman Wright delivered a furious statement. He had not seen the charges against the teachers before the evening at Kheel's office, and he was shocked at the insubstantiality of some of them. Decentralization had been wrecked in Albany by these damned discharges, and the children's school year was being ruined by the resulting strike. Kheel's proposal was an honorable and fair way out of the dispute, and he moved the acceptance of all of it except point four, the payment for the teachers who had struck, which in any event was the business of the Board of Education and not of the governing board. McCoy, who rarely expressed opinions at governing board meetings, and whose image to the outside world was that of a man intent on a fair solution, undertook the reply to Wright. He denounced the Kheel proposal as an establishment trick, compulsory arbitration under a thin disguise, and he urged the members of the board to stick to their resolve that these teachers would never again teach in Ocean Hill. The meeting lasted five hours, and at its end the governing board voted 7–4 (Rev. Oliver in the minority), with four abstentions and four absences (among them, Father Powis), to accept the Kheel proposals.

The next morning a small committee of the governing board met with the Board of Education, Donovan and the UFT. Rev. Oliver led the group, and at no time did he mention the vote of the afternoon before. Instead, he presented a statement that Kheel was acceptable as mediator, that the transferred teachers would never be permitted back in the schools, and that the governing board would not be committed to abide by Kheel's findings. Nobody remembers any details of this crucial meeting, except that Father Powis and Board member Morris Iushewitz got into a slanging match, as they usually did wherever they met. At the end of the meeting at the Board, Rev. Oliver announced to the press, in direct contradiction of the vote the night before, that the governing board had rejected the Kheel proposals. That evening Rev. Oliver made an emotional appeal that the governing board could not negotiate away a community's right to determine who taught its children (bad history, incidentally: what Rev. Oliver was opposing is the definition of public schooling by the state); and with McCoy's help, Wright being absent, he turned the governing board around. On the evening of June 11 the previous day's acceptance of the Kheel proposals was revoked. The strike against the district went on, and Donovan returned the matter to Rivers.

On June 17 a neighborhood group called the Committee for Democratic Education began soliciting signatures on petitions calling for the removal of the governing board and new elections. (Rev. Oliver seemed to doubt their good faith: "Our children," he wrote in a public statement, "have now been stabbed in the back by this belated clamor of those who wish to take our children back to the good old days of educational genocide.") On June 18 the board approved a letter to all striking teachers, informing them that if they did not report to work on Thursday, McCoy as unit administrator would rate them "Unsatisfactory" on grounds of excessive absence and would demand their removal from the district. On June 23 Rev. Oliver called on Donovan to invoke the Taylor Law against the striking teachers. Kheel returned from England on June 24, found nothing to do, and withdrew; and the strike went on. The same day Kheel returned, Roy Wilkins of NAACP denounced the governing board for violating teachers' rights.

In the last weeks of the school year, college and graduate students supervised by experts from the Lou Harris office interviewed 212 parents in the Ocean Hill area, and found them in a state of utter disgust. Some 61 percent thought the schools were worse than they had been before (only 3 percent thought they were better); 38 percent thought they would get still worse (only 20 percent thought they would get better). Negative opinions outweighed positive opinions on the Board of Education (69–24 percent), the unit administrator (44–29 percent), the governing board (47–31 percent), the principals (49–40 percent) and the teachers (58–38 percent). On the specific dispute, 29 percent supported McCoy and the governing board in their effort to oust the teachers, while 24 percent supported the teachers, and the other 47 percent were not sure.

The district was still on strike as the academic year ended. Especially at J-271, where a large part of the eighth grade as well as the ninth grade was to be sent to high school, the one-third of the teachers who continued to work performed prodigies of clerical labors, well into the night. They were somewhat helped by the fact that nearly two-thirds of the parents in the district had stopped sending their children to school at all.

The Lindsay Appointees to the Board of Education
Take Charge of the Problem

As the school year ended, in June 1968, Donovan and his staff took the position that the dispute had passed into the hands of Judge Rivers as trial examiner, McCoy was presenting evidence, and it should be assumed that the governing board would abide by any decision reached on the basis of Rivers' report. Rev. Oliver and McCoy met with Deputy Superintendent Theodore Lang of the bureau of personnel and asked special help in recruiting new teachers for the fall, and the help was given. McCoy, alone among the city's district superintendents (which was, functionally, his status), received invitations to visit the universities where a summer Intensive Teacher Training Program was in progress, to solicit for his district. A special licensing exam was set up for seventy-five teachers McCoy claimed to have recruited in the South, but nobody showed up. Another special exam for substitute teachers was given just for Ocean Hill, at Prospect Heights High School, and the governing board asked that 190 places be made ready; but only 19 showed up. As the summer wore on, the Board stopped giving walk-in exams for substitute teacher licenses—higher salaries, rising idealism, bigger college graduating classes and the special reward of draft exemption for teachers had put an end to the shortage of personnel. But it was still possible for principals who needed someone with a special skill to arrange—on Donovan's countersigning their application—an individual walk-in exam. Thirty such were given in August, nearly all for McCoy.

Members of the Board of Education were even less concerned than the staff about the situation on Ocean Hill, because they had reason to know there wasn't going to be any trouble. As part of the decentralization law finally signed by Governor Rockefeller in mid-June, Mayor Lindsay had been authorized to appoint four new members of the Board of Education, to bring its complement temporarily to thirteen. (As others were about to resign, the Mayor in fact would have a chance to appoint a majority of the thirteen over the next few months.) Among his first choices in mid-July were William Haddad, a former newspaperman and Reform Democrat who was building himself a new career in the poverty program, and Rev. Milton Galamison, an independent, easygoing minister of a Brooklyn Negro church, who had sporadically made himself the center of specific civil rights drives, including two school boycotts in 1963–64 and the People's Board of Education in early 1967. (He had also announced a one-day boycott at seven schools, to support Ocean Hill in May 1968.) In different ways, Haddad and Rev. Galamison could claim Ocean Hill as their constituency, and both told the Board that their sources said the people out there were ready for compromise and the whole dispute was going to work itself out peacefully. "I've been meeting with McCoy and Shanker," Haddad told one meeting of the Board, "and we're right on the edge of an agreement." This being what the Board of Education wanted to hear, everyone believed it.

The reason Haddad and Rev. Galamison thought there was going to be an easy way out was, simply, that McCoy, at least by indirection, had told them so. (McCoy denies their interpretation of what he was saying. "If I'd been an outsider listening to me at those meetings," he commented recently, "and the subject had been the weather, I'd have bought an umbrella and galoshes.") In July, however, McCoy and the governing board had excellent reason to wish to play down the prospects of future conflict. Assemblyman Wright had broken with the governing board over the rejection of the Kheel proposals, and was supporting the group that called for new elections. (Indeed, the Niemeyer Committee in its report to the Board, dated July 30, recommended a new election for one-third of the slots on the governing board "as soon as possible," with the rest to stand for election "in time . . . to participate in the budget-making process for the 1969–70 school year," which would mean early fall.) In the last week of July, Wright presented to the Board a petition for a new election which he claimed had three thousand signatures on it from the district.

On July 31 Rev. Galamison, new Board member Hector Vasquez and John H. Lotz, a former telephone union official and executive of the Health Insurance Plan who was a hold-over from the old Board, were appointed a committee to look into Wright's case. McCoy showed them petitions supporting the governing board which he said contained five thousand signatures (later some of these petitions were thrown, suitably boxed, at members of the Board of Education, during a public meeting). Some of Wright's signatures turned out to be lists of names all in the same handwriting, and the UFT seemed to have been helping him gather them. Lotz, who is highly sensitive to political arguments, decided that Wright was looking for union support for some future election to the state senate or to Congress, and that his petition should be brushed off. At its August 14 meeting the Board of Education voted to reject the Wright petitions and not to hold new Ocean Hill elections until June 1969.

From late July on, Rev. Galamison met regularly with McCoy and Shanker, often at convivial lunches at which the long-range prospects of the unit were discussed. Rev. Galamison's idea was to remove the issue from the narrow focus of ten teachers to the more general question of what the union could do to make Ocean Hill a model; then the teachers could slip back in (or some would not slip back in) fairly easily, as part of a larger agreement. All the meetings were amicable. Though a majority of the governing board had voted that it would never never never take back any of the teachers who struck the district, or any of the teachers who had been dismissed May 7, McCoy did not warn anyone of the danger of total intransigence on his board. And he never told the governing board about his meetings with Rev. Galamison and Shanker.

Throughout these summer months, when the tragedies of the fall were being determined, McCoy alone was in contact with all parties to the dispute.

Out in the great world beyond Ocean Hill, the Board of Education was wrestling to prepare lists of powers which would be handed over to the city's thirty local school boards under the provisions of the new Marchi Law, and on August 14 the Board announced a plan which looked more grandiose than it was, but did proclaim an apparent shift of the power to hire and fire from the central to the local boards. The UFT was, to say the least, concerned about how teachers' working conditions and security might be affected, especially in the light of the Ocean Hill experience.

Again, the work horses for the Board of Education were Lotz and Rev. Galamison. Shanker had a long list of grievance procedures he wanted spelled out in the decentralization plan, and one by one Lotz and Rev. Galamison worked out provisions satisfactory to the union. On the Ocean Hill question, Lotz suggested a compromise on numbers—the Board of Education would order the return to the district of four of the surviving ten who were challenging their transfer, which Shanker had accepted from Kheel, and maybe thirty-five of those who had struck the district. Then on August 26 Judge Rivers handed down his findings, and denied McCoy the right to transfer out *any* of the ten teachers.

Even the union was a little embarrassed at the unfairness of the decision ("*I* could have won cases against at least three of the ten," says one of them. "The problem is that McCoy and his people don't know how to present evidence"). But now the force of law was behind the reinstatement of all, and Shanker could not yield on any and survive as a union leader. Rev. Galamison accepted the need to put all the teachers back in Ocean Hill; the matter was no longer an issue between the Board of Education and the union. It was still, however, very much an issue in Ocean Hill, where the governing board voted not to accept the Rivers findings—thereby drawing the condemnation not only of the *New York Times,* but also of *El Tiempo* and the *Amsterdam News.*

The Storm Gathers over the City

In the last week of August and the first week of September, the new college graduates who had passed walk-in exams as substitute teachers returned to the city and looked for their teaching assignments, and found they had none. At the bureau of personnel, sympathetic junior assistants told them that although there was a city-wide surplus of beginning subs, Ocean Hill still had vacancies. When McCoy and the governing board came to the Hotel Commodore in Manhattan to meet with the Board of Education on Friday, September 6, they were prepared to operate their schools without any of the union teachers. Meanwhile, the delegate assembly of the UFT had voted a city-wide strike for the opening of school on Monday unless an agreement was reached covering the status of union teachers in all decentralized districts, especially Ocean Hill.

The negotiating committee of the Board of Education had been working hard all day on the details of the contract with the union, and everyone had relaxed with a few drinks at dinner. The members of the governing board were shocked to find some of the Board of Education representatives gently liquored; and the Board members were shocked to find that the governing board, far from listening patiently to explanations of why they would have to take the teachers back, remained bitterly adamant that neither the ten involuntarily transferred teachers nor the hundred-odd (the governing board thought two hundred) strikers who wanted to return would ever again be permitted to darken the door of a school on Ocean Hill.

The totally unproductive Friday night session was followed by a totally unproductive Saturday meeting with the UFT (to which several members of the governing board refused to come). Finally Lotz told the governing board that if they didn't take back the teachers, the Board of Education would simply close down their schools until they had agreed to comply, and might dissolve the district as a separate entity.

Sunday all the clans assembled, each in its own room, at City Hall, and Mayor Lindsay met for the first time with the Ocean Hill governing board. They greeted him with a prepared statement, of which the operative sentences were: "Since the legal machinery of this sick society are forcing these teachers on us under threat of closing our schools and dissolving this district, the Board of Education should return to our district any of the teachers who wish to return. Our original decision remains as before. We refuse to sell out. If the Board of Education and the Superintendent of Schools forces them to return to a community who does not want

64

them, so be it." Members of the governing board remember that the Mayor seemed insulted by this statement, and said it should not be presented to him. He volunteered the help of his assistants in rewriting it, and they went off to edit it into something the Mayor could accept. One member of the governing board says scornfully, "He made it say something that was in his mind, not in ours."

What emerged was a statement to the effect that the governing board would not consent to take the teachers back but would consent to being forced to take the teachers back. As the Mayor phrased it, in reporting to the Board of Education the results of his meeting with the governing board, "They will not seek to prevent their return." When the Mayor was asked whether the teachers would be assigned to classrooms, he brushed the question aside, leading members of the Board to believe that this crucial matter had not been discussed. In fact, Lewis Feldstein of the Mayor's office had asked McCoy to pledge that the returning teachers would receive normal assignments, and McCoy had done so, not only to Feldstein but also (Feldstein says) to Vincent McDonnell of the State Mediation Service. McCoy said he could not make such a statement publicly, however, without wrecking himself in the district; and he never told the governing board that he had given such a pledge.

The union was waiting in the Board of Estimate room at City Hall, and Mayor Lindsay let them wait a while. Shanker learned that the Mayor had left the Board of Education without coming to the union's room, and began to lead his people out the door; and the Mayor arrived. "We've settled it," he said. Shanker asked him how he had settled it, and the Mayor said, "They agreed to take the teachers back." Then the Mayor went downstairs to a televised news conference to announce that schools would be open as scheduled on Monday. Rev. Oliver told the cameras that the Mayor was misinterpreting the governing board's position. Shanker told the cameras that there was no contract, that he would recommend a strike to the membership, which would vote that night, and that he did not expect the schools to open as scheduled. The vote to call the strike was 12,021–1,716.

The fact that the strike was illegal under the Taylor Law, which Mayor Lindsay was sure to invoke, was apparently never discussed.

PART III

THE THREE STRIKES

N EARLY 54,000 of the city's 57,000 teachers stayed out on the opening day of school, September 9, and pickets ringed the buildings, carrying signs demanding "JUSTICE FOR TEACHERS." The principals, who had been through this sort of thing the year before (and who were even more threatened by possible arbitrary actions of local school boards under a decentralized program), declared in 80 percent of the city's nine hundred schools that the failure of teachers to report had created unsafe conditions for children, and the buildings were closed. On Ocean Hill a full complement of staff, nearly all nonunion, reported for work; and in the IS-201 complex in East Harlem only nine teachers joined the strike. Because the hundred-odd UFT teachers who had struck in the spring did not come to work, Ocean Hill was authorized by Board of Education rules to pay on a per-diem substitute basis some hundred-odd extra teachers it had "hired" without approval from (or even notification of) the bureau of personnel.

Through the day, the union and the Board of Education worked on contract terms in reasonably amicable negotiations. There was, in any event, no disagreement about the

Ocean Hill part of the deal: the Board would order the teachers assigned to Ocean Hill to "resume their professional duties," with a wistful offer of free transfer to schools in other districts if they preferred to leave. And the Board agreed to pay for their time on the picket lines the three hundred-plus teachers who had struck the district in the spring, a decision which added fuel to the fires on Ocean Hill. The entire grievance procedure of the union contract with the Board, including all city-wide bylaws dealing with disciplinary questions, was extended to bind all local school boards and their administrative staffs. In cases where local boards might wish to dismiss teachers, the contract required submission of charges to a panel of arbitrators, whose decision would be binding. In addition, Donovan sent to all district superintendents and unit administrators a letter giving UFT chapter chairmen, district chairmen and executive committee members what the labor movement calls "superseniority"—that is, complete protection from transfer out of their existing jobs without their consent.

Shanker had also sought an "agency shop," which would require all teachers to pay dues to the union whether or not they were members, and the Board of Education believes that the strike was called more to enforce that demand than for any other reason. No union of municipal employees has such a clause in its contract (though it is an open secret in the labor movement that the city expects to begin granting agency shops in 1969), and the Board was not prepared to give Shanker the triumph of the first agreement of this kind—especially not, as Lotz pointed out at a convivial moment in the negotiations, Rev. Galamison playing piano in the background, as a reward for an illegal strike. The binding-arbitration clause was offered as a *quid pro quo* in return for the union's (temporary) abandonment of the agency-shop demand.

Agreement on this "Memorandum of Understanding" was reached around four in the afternoon on Tuesday, the second day of the strike. At the Board, leadership in meeting the demands of the teachers had been taken by Rev. Galamison, who asked Shanker to give him public credit when recommending the agreement to his members, and Shanker did so gladly: "One of the persons who spent more hours working on a real understanding—and when we have people there who are working, we shouldn't go by the impressions given in the newspapers, we should know it—that person is the Rev. Mr. Galamison." William Haddad acclaimed the memorandum as "the first real step toward decentralization." Mayor Lindsay, too, clearly felt that the dispute was over—indeed, he had said on the first day of the strike that the governing board had "pulled the rug out from Mr. Shanker" by its agreement not to prevent the return of the teachers.

Shanker offered an olive branch to Ocean Hill with a statement that "McCoy and the governing board are trying to do something in that district." But he was less optimistic than the supporters of the governing board that in fact the battle had ended, and the motion offered to the membership in settlement of the strike authorized the UFT executive board to close the city's schools on forty-eight hours' notice without further action by the membership, "in the event the agreements with respect to Ocean Hill–Brownsville are broken."

Once this contract was signed, the governing board's cause was absolutely hopeless: the full weight of the coercive power of the state would have to be applied, if the union insisted, to restore the UFT teachers to the schools. Men like Haddad and Rev. Galamison might be brought to regret what they had said and done (Rev. Galamison even voted against the contract he had negotiated), but the results could not be changed, and further resistance was certain to be self-destructive. Nobody seems to have bothered to tell the governing board of the drastic change in the status of their dispute with the union. "If you've already got a broken foot," McCoy said the other day, "what difference does it make that you get a broken hand, too?"

The Returning Teachers Are Mistreated
on Ocean Hill, and the Second Strike Begins

Mrs. Sandra Feldman went out to Ocean Hill a little before seven in the morning on Wednesday, October 11, and went directly to McCoy's offices. She had always liked him, and she thought he had a "warm, paternal feeling" for her. Her purpose was to plead with him to use all his considerable influence in the district to insure the safe and fruitful return of the UFT teachers. He was noncommittal, but as they sat in his office, with a correspondent from *Time*, the phone kept ringing and he kept telling callers that, yes, the procedures agreed upon the night before were to be put into effect. Mrs. Feldman, who had done more than her share of demonstrating for various CORE chapters, recognized the syndrome and went off to see what might be going on in the schools.

At J-271 a group led by Sonny Carson of Brooklyn CORE, who is widely regarded as terrorist in his inclinations and does nothing to discourage that opinion, had blocked the front door against the returning teachers. Principal William Harris had come out, and with the help of police had escorted the teachers into the building. There he told them, as the other principals were telling the other UFT teachers through the district, to report to the I-55 auditorium for an orientation session with McCoy. When the teachers arrived at the auditorium, they found about fifty Negro men, some wearing helmets, carrying sticks or with bandoliers of bullets, who shouted curses at them. The eighty-three teachers clus-

70

tered in the center of the auditorium, terrified, and McCoy entered. As he started to speak, choruses of jeers from the men drowned him out, and after a few minutes he left. The lights in the auditorium were then flicked on and off, and the teachers were told from the crowd that if they came back to the district, they would be carried out of it in pine boxes. Finally McCoy returned. If the teachers still insisted on returning to the district, he said, they should report to their schools at one o'clock.

The teachers left the auditorium, caucused and decided to go through with what they had come to do. When they reported to their schools again, they found that they had been given no teaching assignments and that there were no time cards for them to punch. J-271 students were encouraged to leave the school, jeering at and in some cases maneuvering as though to assault the entering teachers. Harris locked the teachers into a room for their own protection, and arranged a police escort for them out of the building at two-fifteen. That afternoon the Ocean Hill teachers reported on their experiences to the executive board of the union, which exercised the option in the motion which had ended the first strike, and called for the city's teachers to walk out again on Friday.

The explanation from the Ocean Hill governing board was that the community had risen spontaneously in its wrath to keep the union teachers out. Rev. Oliver said he hoped the community would do it again. Both the Board of Education and the Mayor's office were paralyzed by the crisis. Though the terrorism on Ocean Hill had obviously been prearranged, there was a strong emotional desire at the Mayor's office to accept the governing board's explanations.

Mayor Lindsay tried to withdraw himself from the situation: on Thursday morning he called Commissioner James

Allen in Albany and begged him to come down to City Hall and meet there with the Ocean Hill–Brownsville governing board. Maybe a state takeover, which McCoy had proposed at one point, might solve the problem. Allen explained that as chief state school officer he could not be directly involved in negotiations. (The Mayor met with the governing board himself, and they walked out on him.) Then Donovan called Allen to tell him that the Board of Education had voted 7–1 to request his intervention (Mrs. Shapiro dissenting, on the ground that the Board should first try to manage its own troubles).

Allen drove down to New York and met Thursday night at ten o'clock with members of the Board of Education. He asked them what they wanted him to do, and Rev. Galamison said that they were ten, eleven people, and couldn't agree on anything; he was one person, it would be easier for him. Allen delivered a lecture to the Board, about what a disgrace it was that they couldn't function as a board but were forever leaving meetings to call their constituencies before they were willing to vote on anything. The Board did not disagree. Allen agreed to look for an answer, and spoke briefly the next day with some of the participants. Then he called Ted Kheel, who met with him ten o'clock Friday night, September 13, at the Century Association on West 43rd Street. The union had resumed its strike that morning.

Commissioner Allen Offers and Then Withdraws the First Allen Plan

Kheel told Allen that, frankly, he was reluctant to become involved, and certainly could not accept appointment as a mediator. Mediation implied the existence of a dispute, and here there was a contract, signed, sealed and delivered. The union could properly take the position that the only

72

issue was one of contract enforcement. But it was a trivial dispute, and the need was to cauterize it. The union's leverage was the strike, but if the union won, the result would be that the teachers would be in Ocean Hill every day, essentially at the mercy of the governing board. The district's leverage was its physical control over teachers, but if the district won, the state legislature would throw them and all decentralization projects out of business. The only possible solution was to remove the sources of dispute on both sides—the governing board should be suspended, and the ten teachers transferred temporarily to headquarters assignment.

The next day, which was Al Shanker's fortieth birthday, Kheel invited Shanker to his home in Riverdale and discussed the suggestion he had made to Allen. Shanker said the plan was no good, because the governing board could not in fact be suspended. It would continue to be out there, and to give orders to McCoy. Kheel said that of course it could be suspended, because on any sign of its interference in the district the Board of Education could cut off the funds to the schools. After considerable conversation, Shanker said he thought his negotiating committee might buy it, provided there was a formal agreement that the governing board would never be restored until the ten teachers were taken back, and that McCoy agreed to take his orders from Donovan.

While Kheel and Shanker were conferring, Mayor Lindsay was facing an angry meeting of the city's parents associations at J-104 near Stuyvesant Town in Manhattan. Among other questions he was asked how the governing board could be permitted to continue in office after its clear violation of its agreement not to prevent the return of the teachers. The Mayor said he thought the governing board had lived up to its agreement with him, "more or less," and experienced the

73

first of what were to be several vigorous booings he would receive during the strike. More important, he lost forever any chance to be the guarantor of a strike settlement: the teachers who had been terrorized on Ocean Hill, and all those who spoke to them, would not trust anyone who reacted so calmly to what had happened on September 11 at I-55.

That first Saturday, Allen announced his first Allen Plan, which was Kheel's trade-off of governing board against ten teachers; it was greeted with universal editorial acclaim. On the same day Mayor Lindsay swore in three more new members of the Board of Education—John M. Doar, a former Assistant Attorney General under Robert Kennedy who had prosecuted civil rights cases in the South and had come North to be head of the Bedford-Stuyvesant Development Corporation (within which lay most of the Ocean Hill–Brownsville district); Walter W. Straley, a vice president of AT&T; and Mrs. Maria Conigliaro, a vocal Puerto Rican leader. Almost from the day of his inauguration the Mayor had been saying that his office should have control of the Board of Education. Now for the first time a majority of that Board was of his choice. Nobody congratulated him.

The first act of the new Lindsay majority on the Board of Education was to follow the Allen directive and suspend the Ocean Hill governing board. The union responded that it would take the paired suspension of governing board and teachers only on a provision that the governing board would not be restored until the teachers were in their classrooms—and then added further conditions. The surviving sixty-odd teachers the governing board had rejected would have to be guaranteed classroom assignments, neutral observers would have to be stationed in the schools with power to close them in case of disorder, and the Mayor would have to promise not to approve actions of unofficial groups harassing teachers.

The Ocean Hill governing board reacted in fury—they were a "legal body," Rev. Oliver said, the Board of Education could not unseat them—and sought an injunction first in the state courts and then in the federal courts, most unsuccessfully (the state Appellate Division, which had also heard argument in Assemblyman Wright's petition for a writ to force the Board of Education to hold new elections on Ocean Hill, doubted that the governing board was legitimate even when recognized by the Board of Education, let alone separately "legal"). Kenneth Clark raged at Commissioner Allen for apparently equating the supposed rights of ten teachers with the educational hopes of the Negro community. On September 20 Allen permitted the Board of Education to restore the governing board, which made Clark (and the majority of the Board of Education) happier; but its net effect was to relieve Shanker of any obligation to accept even the temporary transfer of the dismissed ten. Now the union's demand was for suspension of the governing board and *restoration* of all UFT teachers.

The Second Strike Grows Unpleasant and Is Settled

The strike was highly successful and increasingly nasty. Brushing off a plea from the Mayor, the UFT held a mass meeting in front of City Hall on September 16, with something more than fifteen thousand teachers and other unionists in attendance. Though Bayard Rustin and a number of Negro union leaders were present, the crowd was overwhelmingly white. The awkward fact was that McCoy and most of the governing board were Negro, and every one of the ten teachers was Jewish. The Mayor's office had seen this clash as racial from the beginning, and now began to say so. And the UFT began to solicit support with the distribution of leaflets reproducing anti-Semitic literature which had appeared in the Ocean Hill district. As several people have pointed out, the union gave this stuff infinitely more circulation than its producers could have dreamed it would have—and some of it was simply the ravings of a single fanatic with access to a mimeograph machine.*

On Ocean Hill, attendance was light (even with children brought in from other districts, the schools were never so much as two-thirds full), but all classrooms were manned, most of them by enthusiastic beginners who impressed visitors to the district, especially visitors who were also enthusiastic beginners. Seventy percent of the new teachers were white, and half were Jewish; they were a fair sampling of

* The item for which the union was most severely criticized, however, was legitimate. It was a report from the independent journal *Education News* on a class in which a teacher named Leslie Campbell advocated black separatism and Molotov cocktails. The leaflet reported the class as an "actual lesson in J.H.S. 271," and called it an "example of what the Ocean Hill–Brownsville governing board feels is suitable curriculum." The New York Civil Liberties Union called these statements "frauds" and "a lie," because the class in question had been observed elsewhere in the city. But Campbell *was* in J-271, and he had been hired by the governing board subsequent to the publication of the report in *Education News*. So the case was apparently even *stronger* than the UFT leaflet indicated.

If one goes a cut deeper, however, beyond where either the UFT or NYCLU penetrated, it begins to appear that NYCLU did unwittingly expose an unfairness in the UFT literature. Campbell was in the district because he had been punitively transferred from his previous school. Asked where he wanted to go, he said, Ocean Hill. Donovan called McCoy and asked whether he would take Campbell, and McCoy said, "Sure." Considering who Campbell's friends were in the district, it would have been almost impossible for McCoy to say no. Conceivably, of course—once the notion of conspiracy is afoot, anything is believable —McCoy could have set up the request and the telephone call; but one doubts it. That the governing board was not united in its affection for Campbell, however, is a matter of record in its minutes. At the meeting where the dismissal of the nineteen was voted, Mrs. Elaine Rooke, a governing board member sufficiently militant to be among those indicted by a Brooklyn grand jury in December, moved to add Campbell's name to the list of those who must go, and got a second but not a majority. Pity.

what the bureau of personnel had referred to Ocean Hill those last weeks before school opened. Apart from the earlier questions of principle, the Ocean Hill dispute had acquired the most difficult of all strike issues to settle: the disposal of the surplus staff, who had loyally worked for management (or, from the union point of view, scabbed) during the strike. Moreover, Ocean Hill was operating much as its leaders wished: there was no pressure on them to settle. All the pressure was on the rest of the city, where more than a million children were out of school.

The Board of Education kept announcing that schools were open, ordering teachers and supervisors back to them, ordering McCoy and the governing board to receive the UFT teachers back to their classrooms. Nobody paid any attention. The Board appointed John Doar head of a new negotiating committee, which met with Shanker over the weekend of September 21 and 22. Doar questioned whether the Board was still bound by its Memorandum of Agreement, which he thought might have been voided by the strike, and Shanker walked out of the meeting. The next day the rest of the Board and the Mayor's office assured Doar that the school system was, indeed, still bound by the Memorandum.

Accepting that decision, Doar thereafter regarded his mission as one of assuring compliance with law. He had made the University of Mississippi accept James Meredith, and now he would make the governing board of Ocean Hill accept the UFT teachers. For Shanker, however, the question was one of simple labor-relations obligation. He had taken a grievance, and he had won it, and now the boss was permitting middle management to wreck the agreement in a branch office. The Ocean Hill board was not an independent body to be dealt with by persuasion or legal compulsion (Doar talked about injunctions); it was a local manager to be fired if he didn't obey orders. Neither man had ever seen anything

77

quite like the other, and personally they got on very well. Between late September and mid-November, Shanker and Doar dined together at least once a week, hashing out their intellectual disagreements on a rather abstract level.

But the schools were still closed. On September 24, reluctantly, the Mayor put himself back in the picture, meeting with all parties, and the strike began to grind toward settlement. On the twenty-sixth Donovan announced (to the great resentment of the governing board) that he was assigning thirty-seven observers to keep an eye on conditions in the Ocean Hill schools; on the twenty-seventh he announced that the observers would be backed by police, and the union teachers could return safely. That day talks with the union broke down over the issue of union observers in the schools, and the power of the observers to close schools. And on Saturday the twenty-eighth all parties adjourned to Gracie Mansion for one of those all-night sessions which have been since the Wagner days part of the disease of labor relations in New York City.

From the beginning, the elements of the settlement had been obvious. The union teachers were going back—my question to McCoy in May of how big an army would be sent with them was about to be answered with a declaration that the army would be as large as might be needed. Ocean Hill still manfully opposed their return, but Mayor Lindsay for eight hours wore down the governing board's new lawyer, the peppery civil liberties specialist William Kunstler. The city was, however, prepared to sweeten the pot for the project by awarding the district as many extra positions as might be necessary to keep existing staff while taking back the UFT teachers, giving McCoy a unique resource of additional staff to plan and execute new programs.

And the union was going to get authority to station observers of its own choice in the Ocean Hill schools. Though

Shanker trusted nobody to maintain the rights of his teachers, he could live with a situation where the reports of his observers could be used to mobilize public opinion against any use of strong-arm tactics by the governing board. But here the Board of Education was fierce in opposition.

Doar insisted that his observers, whom Donovan had already stationed in the schools, would be all anybody needed. What was required now, he felt, was voluntary compliance by Ocean Hill, which could not be got if the Board seemed to be pushed around by the union. Doar refused to yield to the Mayor on the question of outside observers, and the negotiations went on to other topics.

By dawn's early light on Sunday, Doar, sitting exhausted in a chair, saw Shanker and state mediator McDonnell and Mayor Lindsay's labor adviser Harold Israelson coming down the stairs together and talking about how the children were going to make up the lost time and the teachers the lost paychecks, and how the deductions were to be taken for the weeks of the strike. Shanker was suggesting that one-third of the teachers' monetary loss be deducted from each of the next three paychecks, to minimize hardship, and Doar suddenly sat up straight and said, "To hell with it; I'm not going to give any more." He thereupon departed. Rev. Galamison had left some hours before, as had the Ocean Hill contingent, and AT&T Vice President Walter Straley remained to sign the contract for the Board of Education.

Two Weeks of Turmoil on Ocean Hill Are Followed by Catastrophe

A few peace offerings were made in Ocean Hill's direction that Sunday after the deal was closed. Doar stressed that the Board had managed to avoid a situation where union—or even neutral—observers would be empowered to close a school. And Shanker, selling his deal to his delegate assembly, closed with the words, "Now we shall all have to learn to work with Rhody McCoy." The governing board was silent, apparently too shocked to speak.

School opened Monday with more than a thousand policemen in Ocean Hill, an assistant superintendent from school headquarters in each building, and men from the Mayor's office and the UFT checking up on what was happening. Just outside the district, in P-45, the Board of Education had set up a command post with a battery of telephone lines for an enforcement committee of its members. Doar and Rev. Galamison went into the schools themselves to see what they could do to keep things cool, and Straley handled the operation at P-45.

Virtually no UFT teachers received assignments that first day. Mayor Lindsay called Shanker twice at his office and once at home in the evening to explain that Doar was working on the problem and was confident he could handle it. Shanker, so long as the police guaranteed the physical security of his members, had no reluctance about allowing arrangements to mature. Donovan ordered McCoy to put the returning teachers into classrooms.

Tuesday, October 1, there was a riot in and outside J-271, with ten policemen and an undetermined number of local residents and visiting helpers injured. Elsewhere in the district, however, principals began assigning UFT teachers to real jobs. Donovan ordered J-271 closed for the one day Wednesday, October 2, to allow some time for contemplation. On the Wednesday the governing board met and ordered McCoy to take the UFT teachers out of the classrooms. McCoy put the resolution in his pocket and left it there.

Thursday and Friday were considered hopeful days by the observers. Donovan says two-thirds of the union's teachers had classroom assignments and were teaching (some under a "buddy system" in pairs with the Ocean Hill teachers); Shanker says it was under one-third. J-271, reopened, was still the hot spot. Here UFT teachers were assigned extra lunch-room duty (the most likely place to get in trouble), hall patrol down to and including watching the toilets, textbook inventory work and classes to which no students came, in most instances because the names on the rollbook were the names of children who were absent. As problems were specifically called to his attention, however, principal William Harris took care of them. Sometimes they were much less serious than they looked. A union observer came bursting into Harris' office to say that Sonny Carson had just gone into a teacher's room. Harris took off as though shot from a longbow, to the specified room. Sure enough, Carson was there: he had been in the halls, and the teacher had invited him to come in and debate the issues of the strike before the class. Harris asked Carson to leave anyway, as he had no business in the building, and Carson complied.

On Sunday, October 6, Rev. Oliver told the press that McCoy had orders from the governing board to take all the UFT teachers out of the classrooms. The next morning McCoy denied it, but there was another meeting of the governing board, McCoy attended, and when he came out he said he would have to follow the instructions of his board rather than those of Dr. Donovan. The Board of Education again suspended the governing board. Tuesday, October 8, Donovan and McCoy met with the principals, all but one of whom announced that they would obey the orders of the local leadership. (The one exception was Irving Gerber, who had a career to save in the school system, and he asked for transfer out of the district because his acceptance of Donovan's orders would make him ineffective on Ocean Hill.) McCoy was suspended for telling the principals to remove the teachers and was assigned to headquarters; and then the principals were suspended at the end of the day, after they had ordered the removal of the UFT teachers from classes in their schools; and they, too, were assigned to headquarters. McCoy told them to go, and they did. Their only other appearance in the district that week was with Human Rights Commissioner William H. Booth, who toured the district's schools and brought some of the principals along, identifying them to police as his assistants. Donovan found out about it, and ordered the police to bar them, whether they came with Booth or not.

McCoy, however, remained at his desk in Ocean Hill—still, as Shanker pointed out, drawing his salary. The governing board still met in the same place and issued the same orders (and those members of the governing board who were being paid for their services were still getting their checks from Ford through Queens College). The suspensions had been meaningful only in the case of the principals; and the union leaders noted later that this removal of the principals was the only handhold they had ever, in fact, got on Ocean Hill.

On Wednesday, October 9, J-271 erupted again, with all sorts of angry people in the hallways. The dreary details are not important here—they will be aired, in any event, in criminal court in Brooklyn—but they were bad enough to make the assistant principal, a Negro professional who had seen a lot of schools, ask for her transfer out; and they quickly persuaded Donovan to close the school. He asked the staff, both union and nonunion, to meet with him in one of the Board of Education offices near Brooklyn's Borough Hall, early the next day. McCoy told the staff to go.

Thursday morning Donovan met with about 125 teachers from J-271, and told them that only they could end the trouble in their school. Either they would learn to get along with each other or he would disperse the staff and bring in a new staff. Albert Vann of the African-American Teachers Association said he thought the staff would like to talk over its problems by itself, and Donovan left.

Out on Ocean Hill the assistant principals who had taken charge of the other buildings assigned UFT teachers to classes, and the district was reasonably placid, for an armed camp.

Friday, October 11, the Board of Education held a meeting that was more like a permanent crap game than a session of an official body. Individual members drifted in and out, checking with their constituencies or with the parties to the dispute or making personal phone calls or just walking around. Donovan left the meeting to go talk again with the J-271 teachers and see how they seemed to be doing. A girl who appeared to be a spokesman for the newly hired teachers rose when Donovan asked for news and said she thought everything was going to work out—and then Al Shanker stepped through the doors at the back of the room and leaned against the wall.

"Why don't you have *him* arrested?" bellowed Leslie Campbell, but the other teachers shushed him.

Donovan asked Shanker to leave, and he refused. His people had told him they were concerned that Donovan might push them around, and he wanted to be there to be sure it didn't happen. Donovan explained that it was a private meeting, and Shanker said that he had a right to be at any meeting which the Superintendent held with union teachers. Donovan said icily that he did not equate the post of Superintendent of Schools with that of president of the United Federation of Teachers, and Shanker shrugged. Donovan said that unless Shanker left he would leave, and Shanker stayed. When Donovan left, Shanker followed, and Donovan stopped him. "What's got into *you*, Al?" Donovan said. "I don't know that they can work it out, but this is the best chance we've had." Shanker stubbornly insisted that his people might be bullied in his absence. Donovan said he was going to return to the room, and Shanker said that if he did, Shanker would go along. Donovan quit, and the two men left in different directions.

Donovan went back to a conference room right next to his office, where the seven suspended principals were waiting for him. He told them he was going to put them back into the district, but that if they goofed off, if there were any outsiders rampaging in the halls or union teachers interfered with or children stimulated to make trouble, he would not just suspend them—he would fire them, and make it hard for them to get jobs elsewhere. Nobody said much, but Donovan was sure the message had sunk in.

The Superintendent then proceeded back to where some of the Board were meeting, and reported on his day (mentioning that presently he had to be up and doing, for he was to catch a plane for Denver to make a speech). Rev. Galamison said he had spoken with the suspended principals, and they had given *him* a pledge that they would treat all teachers alike, and that all would be quiet at J-271. Doar talked to McCoy, who assured him that, governing board or no governing board, the teachers would be given real assignments the next day if the principals were restored. You just couldn't ask them to make a public statement ("rub their nose in it," Rev. Galamison said). The members of the Board at the meeting were furious with Shanker for barging in on Donovan's session with the J-271 teachers, and they were in a rush. In this mood, a rump committee of the Board—different accounts speak of four, five or six members, certainly less than a quorum—told Donovan to order J-271 reopened and the principals reinstated, as of Monday. Donovan gave a statement to the press, and departed for Denver.

Shanker learned what had happened when reporters called him for his reaction, and he instantly set in motion the machinery for calling a third strike. Before Donovan's plane had set down in Denver, Mayor Lindsay's office had called every possible stopping place in that city to reach him, and to tell him to come home. Saturday was a day of hardening positions. First thing Sunday morning, Mayor Lindsay called Mrs. Shapiro, in her last innings as president of the Board (it had already been leaked that Doar would be elected to the post the following week, and that Rev. Galamison, saints preserve us, would become vice president). The Mayor asked Mrs. Shapiro to call a meeting of the Board for that Sunday afternoon. Mrs. Shapiro refused—she had seen enough meetings of the Board to last her quite a while—but she put together a smaller meeting of herself, Donovan, Shanker, Harold Siegel (the secretary of the Board), Harold Israelson and Deputy Mayor Robert Sweet, to gather that afternoon in her apartment on lower Fifth Avenue.

First, though, Donovan and Sweet met with Israelson, the Mayor's labor adviser, at *his* apartment, and Donovan admitted that he had not received a pledge of cooperation from the principals: he had simply told them what they were going to do, and they had not denied it. Nor could he be completely confident of what would be done by the J-271 staff, which contained what everybody (including the Ocean Hill administrators and governing board) considered some thoroughly disreputable elements in terms of politics or thuggery. He told Sweet that he felt the Friday announcement had been premature, and that everything should be retained *in statu quo* for at least one more day.

This option was not offered to Shanker, however, at the meeting in Mrs. Shapiro's apartment. Doar, who had been less than enthusiastic about Friday's announcement but had gone along with Rev. Galamison, now argued sensibly that to keep J-271 closed after the announcements would be to knuckle under to the union, and would foreclose any chance of the Board's establishing itself as a neutral authority not only on Ocean Hill but elsewhere in the city. The most that could be offered Shanker was a public guarantee from Donovan.

Shanker, who had been discussing the prospective third strike with his delegate assembly, arrived late, and began by trying to find out from Donovan what had happened Friday. Donovan told him what he had told Israelson and Sweet (*not* including his recommendation that the Friday decision be revoked), and offered to get on the telephone now, call the seven principals and secure from each of them an absolute pledge that the union teachers would be free from harassment and would get teaching assignments. Anyone who wouldn't pledge wouldn't be reinstated. But the fact is that Donovan was not selling the deal. He was vague about how much leeway the principals would have in assigning UFT teachers to nonteaching chores. Asked for his personal rather than his official views, he told Shanker that he thought things would be kept cool on Monday and probably Tuesday, but that later in the week hell would probably break out again. Now Shanker suggested that J-271 be kept closed and the principals be kept suspended for just one more day, while arrangements for controlling the reopenings and reinstatements were perfected. He was told that was impossible.

Still, the discussions did move. Shanker was willing to admit that the principals would find it next to impossible to issue public statements that they would assign *all* the union teachers. Donovan offered to make the public statement himself, after talking with them. People began suggesting wordings for Donovan's statement, and Sweet called the Mayor to tell him the situation looked promising. Then Shanker suddenly shook his head and said it wasn't enough: he was not ready to ask his people to remain on the job on the strength of nothing more than a statement by Donovan that third parties had said something or other to him. Sweet suggested that Shanker get his strike authorization and keep it in readiness in case the pledges to Donovan proved delusory, but Shanker had now made up his mind. There could be no question that his people would follow him; the city was in terrible trouble.

One last clear chance remained to avoid catastrophe: the Board of Education could revoke Donovan's statements of the previous Friday and give Shanker and Donovan the day to work out something formal with signatures down at the bottom. Having failed to persuade Mrs. Shapiro to call a meeting of the whole Board, Mayor Lindsay had got Rev. Galamison to call a rump meeting of the Lindsay appointees, who came together for dinner that Sunday night at Armando's Restaurant in Brooklyn. Sweet and Donovan went over to City Hall from Mrs. Shapiro's apartment and called Armando's. Conscious of all the problems that might follow, both men (Sweet speaking for the Mayor) begged the seven new members of the Board to abandon Friday's position. Israelson warned Doar separately that if the union did strike again, any subsequent settlement would be worse, from the Board's and from Ocean Hill's point of view, than what was in the existing contract.

History moves at its own pace; time gallops withal. But one should pause here, at this instant of truly fateful decision, to consider those in whose hands the future of the city was now placed. Six of the seven were in one way or another intimately connected with poverty programs or with "promoting social change." They were, to be marginally unkind, fundamentally in the resentment business: that is, their function was to push on those who made decisions, not to make decisions themselves. Though it was fashionable to say they had "constituencies," in fact they did not; they had been elected to nothing and they were responsible to no one except for their performance as spokesmen for a position. Their habit was to deal with issues, not with people. None of the six really understood how a big organization runs; the fragility and interdependence of *normal* urban life were something they had no way to think about, because their work dealt entirely with pathologies. The man who had to run the school system and the man who had to run the city now came to this group, recently placed in brief authority over the one by appointment of the other, and pleaded with them to take the one action that could avoid catastrophe for the city. The six had no way to think about the situation except in terms of slogans and personalities and the positions they had taken. Worst of all, they were to make their decisions in secret, for the Mayor's office would shield them. These pages are the first appearance in print of the fact of the meeting at Armando's Restaurant on the night of October 13.

The seventh man in the group, Walter Straley of the telephone company, had the background and training and position to see how profoundly harmful a third teacher strike would be. For five hours, from seven to midnight, he hammered at his colleagues to get them to reverse the decision to reopen J-271, which they had so hastily taken on Friday. He could not budge one of them.

The Mayor on television spoke in agony about Shanker and the teachers' union, about the closing of all the city's schools over a dispute in one of them, about the lack of "moral authority" in the union to do what it was doing. (He reversed reality a little by saying Donovan was asking Shanker for one day to make his plan work, when it had been Shanker asking Donovan for one day to get a plan written.) It is no defense of Shanker, who with the third strike moved his union from a posture of defending its own to a posture of attacking the poor people of Ocean Hill, to say that he was honestly acting in what he considered the best interests of those who had chosen him to make such decisions for them. But it is perhaps a valid defense of the old, supposedly discredited ethnic politics to point out that in a city two-thirds non-Spanish Catholic and Jewish, the political decision to permit the horror of the third teacher strike was taken by a group which did not include a single representative of the two majority elements, and which acted solely on the basis of the ideological bias and self-esteem of its members.

Fewer than eight thousand teachers now voted to commit the union to the third strike; and on October 14 fifty thousand-odd were again out of the schools, demanding now an end to the Ocean Hill project.

The Third Strike Corrodes
the Morale of the City

On their third strike the teachers stayed out for five weeks. Though the Board of Education and the newspapers kept making optimistic noises about schools in operation despite the strike, at no time were as many as an eighth of the city's schoolchildren in school. In September the union had commanded the sympathy certainly of a majority of the city's residents and perhaps of a majority of parents. By the end of the third strike parents were frantic and furious. Perhaps it may be noted here without comment that none of the principal figures—not Shanker, not McCoy, not Doar, not Mayor Lindsay, not McGeorge Bundy—had children in the New York City public schools. And perhaps it should also be noted that all the children of these worthies, and of the teachers, are well fed at home, while for tens of thousands of colored children in New York the free school lunch they now missed was the one good meal they ate.

The Mayor's first reaction to the new strike was to try to

nationalize the dispute, and to secure mediation by three figures whose work was fundamentally outside New York—John Gardner of the Urban Coalition, Whitney Young of the National Urban League and George Meany of the AFL-CIO. Thought being equal at the Mayor's office to press release, the public knew that the Mayor was trying to gather up this committee at about the same time the Mayor learned that of the three only Young was prepared to serve. The Mayor then put together a more local group, keeping Young, and substituting Harold Israelson and Ted Kheel for Gardner and Meany. Kheel agreed to be a fact-finder only, because there was nothing to mediate—there were now *two* contracts here, beyond any mediator's poor power to add or detract.

Meanwhile, the Board of Education had elected John Doar its new president, and Doar had made a few statements which seemed to mean that the Board was honest-Injun going to try to break a strike by the largest union local in the United States. The response from the labor movement—taken without even consulting Shanker—was quick. On a suggestion from the national AFL-CIO and the Central Labor Council, the custodians' union instructed its members to shut off the power and the boilers and close and lock the schools. In some instances the custodians thoughtfully changed the locks, so nonstriking principals and school officials could not get in.

Having failed to gain an injunction against the Board of Education in the state courts, Ocean Hill now went to federal court for an order which might bar its suspension. The matter was heard by Judge Anthony Travia, who noted with interest that he had all the parties to the dispute in his courtroom. He suggested that they all meet together in his chambers and see if they couldn't work things out, as litigants often do, in pretrial sessions.

The discussion in Travia's chambers on October 18 set the

stage for the eruption of ill feeling that characterized the last weeks of the strike. Nearly all the governing board attended, sitting in ranks suspiciously at the back of the room and glaring at Shanker and Donovan. At this meeting the governing board for the first time suggested that it might consent to take the teachers back. After all, its new counsel Morton Stavis said, the Board of Regents was about to approve new decentralization rules proposed by the Board of Education pursuant to the Marchi Law. Under these rules a district would be empowered to transfer out anybody without reason, provided only it could find another district willing to accept the transferred teacher. Thus Shanker's teachers could be batted back and forth between, say, Ocean Hill and its friends at IS-201. Rev. Oliver cheerfully agreed. Thereafter Shanker, who would have been deeply suspicious anyway, was never willing even to consider any apparent concession offered by Ocean Hill.

Mayor Lindsay Seeks a Simple Answer, and Whitney Young Looks for Good Faith

That first weekend of the third strike, Kheel, Young and Israelson met with the people who had been in Travia's chambers, and reported back gloomily to the Mayor that it looked like a long strike. Around the city, in an obviously desperate gesture, parents and nonstriking teachers, urged on by Rev. Galamison, broke into some of the schools the custodians had closed. Everywhere, attitudes were growing ever more ugly.

The Mayor decided that the focus of the situation was J-271; the Board had made a mistake in reopening it; now the Mayor would close it. Mayor Lindsay met with Deputy Inspector Lloyd Sealy, who was in charge of the army of

91

occupation on Ocean Hill, and asked how much trouble would result from closing J-271 by executive order. Sealy said there would be plenty of trouble; people in the district had not been upset when the school was closed before, because they knew what viciousness had been displayed inside it. But now the school was functioning, on the governing board's terms, and closing it would be seen as deliberate, cold-blooded punishment of the community. Still, if need be, his men could control the area.

The Mayor then asked the deputies from the other boroughs how greatly the wave of school break-ins was stretching their resources, and they said they were in trouble. The police situation was complicated by the recent rejection of the policemen's own labor contract, with a resulting "job action" which was depleting the force. The Mayor decided to close J-271 on his own authority as the city's "Chief Magistrate," in hopes that this action would end the strike. He drove down to Brooklyn, where the Board of Education was meeting in executive session, and told the Board what he was going to do. Some members asked if he objected to their voting on it, which he did not, though he wanted it understood that he would proceed on his own course whatever the vote was. The Board voted against closing J-271, but not, the Mayor thought, passionately. He then returned to Gracie Mansion, called in the television crews and made his announcement.

Shanker, Commissioner Allen, Kheel, Young and Israelson all learned of the Mayor's action from the news media, and were not amused. The union rejected the Mayor's initiative, and Ocean Hill seethed with feelings of betrayal.

But the Mayor's announcement had revealed to Whitney Young—angry as he was about it—how little support Ocean Hill enjoyed outside the Negro community, and how seriously endangered decentralization was by the governing board's recalcitrance on the issue of the UFT teachers. In May the Urban League had joined with other members of the Interracial Colloquy to urge binding arbitration of the dispute over the nineteen dismissed educators. But Young had been moved by the strike, and infuriated by the union's use of anti-Semitic literature from the likes of Ralph Poynter, a "militant" who was, Young said, equally unknown in the Negro and the white communities. Both in an Urban League advertisement on the strike and in an interview, Young had shifted to support the governing board's action in dismissing white teachers without evidence. Negroes, he said, had an "historic, intuitive sense" of who was prejudiced against them, and whites should not question it.

Young now claimed a hearing from the Ocean Hill community, and a meeting was hastily arranged. He told the governing board and parents that the cause of decentralization and community control was suffering nationally because of the New York strike. Hard as it was for them, they would have to take the teachers back. In fact, this decision had already been reached locally, perhaps honestly, perhaps on the theory Stavis had propounded in Travia's chambers. The statement of acceptance, in any event, had been drafted by Father Powis, the most aggressive and abusive figure on the governing board. Now Young was used as a sounding board for it. He was delighted, and so was McCoy, who issued an independent statement of praise for his board.

Shanker, remembering Stavis' argument about the effect of the new decentralization rules, was not even interested in hearing the news Young brought back from Ocean Hill. Young shortly thereafter discussed with Shanker his reasons for skepticism, and offered to stand personal guarantor of the deal. Shanker said that after Young's statements in his ad and interview Shanker could not go back to his membership and say Young was guarantor; and Young explained that he had got the idea of an historic, intuitive sense of who is prejudiced by listening to his Jewish friends, who told him they could tell an anti-Semite at sight. Shanker agreed; he was Jewish, he said, and he thought he could tell an anti-Semite at sight—but that didn't mean he would consider such an intuition a valid reason for depriving a man of his job. On November 1 Young would resign from the Mayor's fact-finding panel (not bothering to notify the Mayor first), and would denounce Shanker for creating "racial strife."

Commissioner Allen Writes an Emancipation Proclamation

This second week of the third strike was the week of initiatives. The Mayor and Young having failed, the State Board of Regents and Commissioner Allen took a try. As the ultimate legal authority for education in the state, the Regents had been under enormous political pressure from Governor Rockefeller and state legislators. Now in their monthly meeting in Albany, on Thursday, October 24, they came to grips with the strike. One of the upstate Regents said that these things never got settled publicly—which everyone had been trying to do that week—and the time had come to settle the strike privately. By unanimous vote, the Regents asked one of their number, Max J. Rubin, a lawyer who was once president of the New York City Board of Education and had negotiated with Shanker, to go down to New York and check out the union's real demands. Fellow Regent Kenneth Clark volunteered to share the limousine with Rubin, and to look in on the Ocean Hill side of the dispute.

Rubin met for two and a half hours with Shanker at the National Arts Club on Gramercy Park, and Shanker made the offer he would repeat that Sunday night in an hour-long television debate with Doar: the union would drop its demand for the removal of the governing board and McCoy, and would settle for the status quo of the last day school was open—everybody on Ocean Hill suspended and J-271 closed. This was not, really, much of an offer; with the principals out of the schools and the assistant principals operating under Donovan's orders, little if anything would be left of the Ocean Hill project. Still, it looked like a step forward.

Rubin was impressed in his conversation with Shanker by the depths of Shanker's distrust of everyone in city government and at school headquarters. He drove back to Albany, found the Board of Regents at dinner and reported on the substance of his conversation with Shanker. Allen seemed troubled by Rubin's presentation of Shanker's argument; and Rubin, who is not well and had had a hard day, was a little irritated about the Commissioner's assumption that he was leaning to the union's side. Everybody went to bed unhappy.

The next morning Allen read to the Regents a statement he had drafted after the previous night's meeting. It stressed the "long history of oppression" the Negro has suffered, and "commitments we cannot abandon, either as a matter of educational policy or as a matter of conscience." Most of the Regents were not entirely sure what these sentiments meant in terms of the New York strike, but they were touched by the depth of Allen's feeling, and with only minor changes the memorandum was adopted as a Regents' statement. Specifically, Allen proposed that the now seventy-nine teachers go back, that the governing board and McCoy be officially restored to office, that they agree to receive the teachers and give them classroom assignments, and that Allen himself or a designee would stand ready to enforce the agreement, up to and including the dismissal (*not* suspension) of anyone who interfered with it. The Regents then called a meeting for five o'clock that afternoon, Friday, October 25, at the Hotel Commodore in New York, with all parties present. The earlier idea of settling the strike privately had been abandoned.

Like most unprepared meetings, the four-way session at the Hotel Commodore went badly, and it ended particularly badly when a group of angry supporters of the governing board entered, and shouted curses and obscenities at the union, Board of Regents and Board of Education alike. The Regents had not been exposed to this sort of thing before, and it made an unfortunate impression. Shanker made an unfortunate impression, too, when he replied to a conciliatory statement by one of the parent members of the governing board with a flat statement that he did not believe she was telling the truth. Anyway, the second Allen Plan was launched, and became a basis for negotiation among the parties. Whitney Young hailed Allen's statement as "a second emancipation proclamation."

Commissioner Allen Meets the UFT Halfway with a Third Allen Plan

On Saturday the twenty-sixth Allen and Shanker and Rubin met for three and a half hours in Allen's suite at the Hotel Commodore, while the Regent and the Commissioner tried vainly to sell the union leader something which his membership was almost certain to see as a step backward. Listening to Shanker's replies, Allen was especially struck with the union's unwillingness to trust either the Mayor or the Board of Education to enforce an agreement in Ocean Hill, and with Shanker's concern about what might happen elsewhere in the city after the end of the strike. The following Tuesday afternoon, the twenty-ninth, Allen attempted to remove some of the union's worries with a detailed proposal sufficiently different from what he had said before to qualify as yet a third Allen Plan; and this plan did, indeed, two and

96

a half weeks later, become the centerpiece of the settlement that ended the strikes.

In the new plan, the state instead of being a remote guarantor of peace on Ocean Hill became the direct administrator of the project. Allen proposed to put the unit under state trusteeship, with a full-time state trustee supported by a full-time staff of state assistants to assume daily oversight in the Ocean Hill schools. Observers, including union observers, would also be present in the schools, and would report back to the trustee rather than to Donovan. The suspension of the governing board would be continued, and McCoy would be reinstated only if he would pledge to follow the orders of the state trustee, regardless of what the governing board (in exile) might say.

Allen called for all parties to accept his new plan by noon on Wednesday, and that morning he met with a very unhappy delegation from Ocean Hill who could not understand why they were so much worse off on Wednesday than they had been on Friday. Ultimately, the governing board decided that it would neither accept nor reject the plan, which meant, functionally, acceptance. The Commissioner's office believes that Shanker, too, was ready to accept—but that his negotiating committee, which knew Allen only as an antagonist on decentralization and as the author of the previous Friday's statement, would not go along.

On November 1 the delegate assembly of the union rejected the Allen plan as "paper promises"; it was the gloomiest day yet. In despair, the Mayor called for the parties to accept arbitration of the issues—which were not now the return of the teachers (let alone the power of the governing board to exclude teachers without giving reasons), but the right of the governing board to survive and to have the principals of its choice in its schools. There is some reason to believe that Shanker had informally accepted this proposal before the

97

Mayor, who had grown wary, announced it; but in the end the union, like everybody else, turned it down. The Mayor reacted with a savage attack on Shanker and the union, and an announcement that what Shanker was really doing was seeking to force a special session of the state legislature, which would almost certainly kill school decentralization in New York.

On November 3 Shanker made the announcement Mayor Lindsay had predicted: the union was calling for a special session. With this gesture Shanker forfeited the support of the Negro union leaders, because he had promised them that he would not seek to kill decentralization, an issue to which much of the Negro community has, perhaps unwisely, made a strong emotional commitment. On November 4 Doar, Donovan, Allen, Mayor Lindsay and Joseph W. McGovern, chancellor of the Board of Regents, issued a joint statement endorsing the Allen Plan and rejecting any possible special session of the legislature.

Tuesday was election day, and the custodians went back to work in the schools. They remained on the job thereafter, easing the tasks of those who were seeking to keep schools open. The picket lines grew more abusive of nonstriking teachers. (There probably was, and is today, as much verbal harassment of nonstrikers by UFT members as there has been of teachers on strike by parents and community representatives. Many teachers who continued to teach during the strike—including Bernard Donovan's daughter—doubt that they will be able to remain in the schools. They do not, of course, have a union to defend their interests.) In certain areas, most notably Bay Ridge in Brooklyn, the union mobilized mass picketing to prevent the reopening of schools. Sentiment in the city began to change: the teacher strikes had become a bad dream that people hoped to find gone each morning when they woke up, please.

A Gimmick and an Indirect Trusteeship
for All City Schools Bring an End to the Strike

In this fourth week of the strike, nobody in the Board of Education, the Mayor's office or the Commissioner's office could see how it could ever be settled at all. Kheel came around rather wistfully with a scorched-earth plan—governing board, McCoy, principals and all disputed teachers to be removed permanently from Ocean Hill. Shanker was not interested.

The fact was that the strike had gathered its own momentum, and was no longer directed against Ocean Hill. It had become nihilist, an expression of the teachers' distrust of the Board, the Mayor and the Commissioner. Max Rubin, surveying the situation with experience as well as distaste, called Allen with the idea that finally produced the settlement—an independent instrumentality without the political (or social) interests or obligations of the public officials, which would be created strictly to maintain the rights of the teachers in the New York schools, and which would be empowered to close any school where these rights were violated. Max Rubin suggested a three-man panel consisting of a Regent, John Doar and an appointee of the Mayor, but Allen thought Shanker would feel that the Mayor dominated any such panel. Rubin's idea of an independent body—a State Supervisory Commission, as it came to be called—was undoubtedly right, but its composition would have to be negotiated with the union rather than imposed by the Commissioner.

Quite independently, the Mayor had called in Shanker, Walter Degnan of the Council of Supervisory Associations and Harry Van Arsdale of the Central Labor Council, and had offered to place in their hands the Chief Magistrate's power to close schools which he had asserted in the J-271 fiasco three weeks earlier. Over the weekend before the fifth week, Rubin's proposal coalesced with the Mayor's gesture of despair, and the outlines of the final settlement—state trusteeship for Ocean Hill, State Supervisory Commission for the rest of the city—began to become clear. But another week of hatred in the streets and name-calling on television was necessary before the deal in fact came into being.

During that interval, on Thursday, November 14, the Appellate Division handed down a 3–2 opinion upholding Justice Rinaldi's decision that the Ocean Hill principals had been appointed illegally, and the Mayor had something else to give the union. The three principals directly involved in this case would be suspended, supposedly pursuant to rule of law, until the Court of Appeals uttered a final ruling; the other Ocean Hill principals would continue on the job. Though Shanker and the union had no real objection to two of the three principals involved, they had become the symbol of the victory the leader could take home to his member- ship—and of the further defeat that the state trustee would now make Ocean Hill swallow.

And again on a Saturday, November 16, at the end of the fifth week of the third strike, everyone in the story gathered at Gracie Mansion—Ocean Hill in the front room, the old part of the mansion; the union on the ground floor in the new back wing; the Board of Education and the Commissioner in the basement of the new wing, where the Mayor has his office. Ted Kheel was lunching with Kenneth Clark at Pavillon, and they were developing a plan by which the Central Labor Council and Clark's MARC could meet together and create a decentralization proposal everyone could live with. Kheel called the Mayor to tell him about the idea, and was informed that a deal was in the making; and the two men went up to the mansion to help out.

Several separate negotiations were in progress.

One was between the union and the Board of Education, essentially Doar and Straley and Donovan, over the contents of the "laundry list," the schedule of longer days and make-up days which would enable children to catch up on missed lessons and teachers to collect missed paychecks.

Another was on the composition and authority of the State Supervisory Commission.

A third was on the details of Allen's statement establishing a state trusteeship on Ocean Hill.

And a fourth, wholly separate, really not a negotiation at all, was the effort by the Mayor and Allen and their deputies, and Kenneth Clark and Whitney Young, to persuade the governing board to go peacefully, to accept the inevitable and trust Allen's and Doar's and the Mayor's goodwill to build back their influence in the schools of their district. But since May the governing board had turned down too many deals infinitely better than this one. Left with a choice between denouncing a sellout and admitting they had been wretchedly ill-advised and wrong since May, the governing board humanly denounced the sellout, and left. On the way out, Father Powis called, "Hey, baby, now we burn down Brooklyn"; and Whitney Young said bitterly, "It's a pity, isn't it, that there are only two thousand blacks you can get killed on Ocean Hill."

Clark moved down to the basement to be with the Mayor and Allen and Doar, to try to keep a voice for Ocean Hill sounding in the cacophony. Kheel ran upstairs and down between officialdom and the union, bearing little pieces of paper with clauses written on them. Nobody was keeping track of what had been and had not been settled. The teachers picked nits of language off the documents, and Kheel and Israelson patiently rewrote.

Finally there were only two issues left: banning the members of the suspended governing board from visiting any schools in the district other than the one in which the individual member had her own children, and removing from the Board of Education decentralization plan the clause which permitted local boards to transfer teachers out involuntarily provided only that some other local board would take them.

Clark pleaded that a contract which barred the governing board from its own schools would be an intolerable humiliation. Shanker in the other room was adamant; it had been members of the governing board who had made the most trouble in the schools during the period of the previous settlements. The compromise worked out was that there would be nothing in any contract to forbid the governing board access to its own schools, but Allen would include such an order in his letter establishing the trusteeship.

Then the negotiations got stuck, surprisingly, on the transfer clause in the new decentralization plan. Doar absolutely refused to budge on the issue. It dawned on the participants that a lawyer's logic had led Doar to the notion that the whole impact of the ten-week troubles could be negated if only a rule were allowed to stand, and everyone, including Clark, turned on him angrily. Finally Doar urged a compromise by which the Board would agree that local boards could not transfer people until after December 31, and his colleagues had him on the ropes. If he was willing to change his document to put a time on it, then no issue of principle could be involved. And was he prepared to give the union the right to strike on this issue after December 31? "You're just trying to get me to go along with the union," Doar complained, but he yielded.

If there had been any ambiguity in the union contract which gave the advisers to the Ocean Hill board the notion that the governing board could successfully stage a confrontation on the issue of involuntary transfer, that ambiguity was now gone. Involuntary transfer had been made a grievance, subject to the full grievance procedures including arbitration. "Pending such decision," the clause concludes, "the status quo of the employee shall be maintained."

Finally, a little after ten in the morning on November 17, twenty-four hours after negotiations had started, the settlement was ready for release. It consisted of two pages of agreement between union and Board, and six pages of letter from Commissioner Allen. While the city waited to learn whether its ten-week agony was over, while the exhausted participants in the negotiations dragged about Gracie Mansion trying to keep awake (Donovan read a detective story), the clerical staff of the Mayor's office took three and one-half hours to type eight double-spaced pages. Nobody's fault, of course: it's the urban crisis.

Why Us?

In real life, of course, there is plenty of fault here.

First, blame lies on the foundations and the Mayor's office for their romantic view of confrontation techniques and their rigidity in maintaining that view even as the destruction spread. In an article on Ocean Hill in the August–September *Interplay,* based entirely on information from within the project, Richard Karp wrote that the governing board had dismissed the teachers with the "tacit approval" of the Mayor's office and "the 'establishment.' " There is some reason to suspect that this statement is true.

Speaking of their April meetings with the governing board —which they had never mentioned publicly until I called to check up on complaints about nonsupport which I had heard in Ocean Hill—the members of the Urban Coalition education task force regretted not their failure to dissuade the governing board from its suicidal action of May 7 but their

103

subsequent success in convincing McCoy that he would have to prefer charges, thus revealing the arbitrary and deliberately provocative nature of what had been done. Now—*now!* —foundation executives are beginning to speak of the troubles they had in the South with projects Rev. Oliver was associated with as part of the Southern Christian Leadership Conference. Before now everybody lay doggo.

The Ford Foundation, which could easily have uncovered the truth about the May 7 action of the governing board, released a pending grant to Ocean Hill–Brownsville at the end of May (and moneys from that grant were paid continuously to the governing board and some of its members as individuals through all the suspensions imposed by the Board of Education and the Commissioner).

None of its large collection of big-time white advisers ever warned the governing board that two can play at the game of confrontation, and that in any direct conflict with the labor movement Ocean Hill would take a fearful beating.

Second, blame lies on the Board of Education both for failing to respond to the anguish of the constructive elements on the governing board in the fall of 1967 and for incompetently failing to find a reasoned response to confrontation in the spring of 1968. The Ocean Hill governing board was and is a creation of the Board of Education, upon whom the parent body could have mandated compulsory arbitration by simple exercise of its rule-making powers. Decentralization is a viable idea only if the plan includes arrangements for some higher authority to assume effective trusteeship over a seriously erring local board. The simplest and least painful way to enforce such a rule would have been to announce that unless the Board of Education were convinced that all teachers in Ocean Hill would be protected against the sort of casual injustice that had been perpetrated on May 7, the bureau of personnel would refuse to assign to the district new teachers to replace those who were surely going to leave. This option was available at least until July.

Later in the summer, the Wright petitions and the Niemeyer Report gave the Board an excellent chance to hold new elections, which would have forced the more radical elements on the governing board to adopt more accommodating tactics or suffer the accusation that they were recreating the conditions of the spring.

Finally, the disorders of the first Wednesday and the union response to them gave the Board of Education a clear choice between keeping the schools closed on Ocean Hill and watching Shanker close them everywhere else in the city. Inertia, as usual, won, penalizing 1,150,000 children, rewarding and encouraging the terrorist elements in Ocean Hill—and ultimately, of course, leaving the governing board much worse off than it would have been if the Board of Education had lowered the boom on September 12 and announced that the Ocean Hill schools were going to be closed until the governing board cooperated in the reinstatement of the union teachers.

Third, blame falls on Mayor Lindsay, whose drive to politicize the school system has been quite exclusive of any thought to the reaction such politicization might provoke— and whose devotion to his much-advertised Urban Task Force has left him increasingly at the mercy of a secret service which gains rewards to the degree it can convince its chief that his state is insecure.

In the controversy over decentralization, the Mayor insisted on treating the teachers as just another pressure group, rather than as the only adults who spend all day in schools. (It is said these days around the Ford Foundation, truthfully or otherwise, that Bundy wanted a UFT representative on his Advisory Committee, and the Mayor vetoed it.) In the spring, when the Ocean Hill situation blew up, the Mayor used his influence to work against decisive action to control and localize the dispute—and in the fall he panicked, saying increasingly harsh things about the union in public and offering increasingly grave concessions in private.

Underlying the third strike was the ugly fact that the teachers' union and the Central Labor Council were not prepared to accept the Mayor's word, or even his signature on a document, as a pledge of his future actions. Not until the three-man State Supervisory Commission had been created to police the agreement—meaning that the teachers would not under any circumstances have to deal with Mayor Lindsay or his appointees if they felt their rights had been violated—would the union agree to end the strike.

The crazy part of it was that the teachers were wrong— that the Mayor on that key Sunday before the third strike was on their side, calling upon his appointees to give Shanker the day the union needed to back away from its strike call. But Shanker knew no more than the newspapers did about the morning meeting of Donovan, Israelson and Sweet, or the dinner at Armando's Restaurant. And nobody outside Ocean Hill knew what the real attitude of the principals would be if they were restored to their jobs the next day.

At the interface between the white world and Ocean Hill stood Rev. Milton Galamison and Rhody McCoy, assuring everybody that everything was going to be all right—which was just exactly what they had been saying, most inaccurately, for months. I have acquired the feeling from browsing around Ocean Hill that this time they may have been right. The neighborhood was not at all happy about the fun and games being played around J-271; and just as the governing board would vote unanimously after the third settlement that Rev. Oliver should not force himself into J-271 after the state trustee had barred him, the parents of the children were probably eager in October to see peace return to their schools. Of course, Rev. Oliver went anyway on the subsequent occasion and got himself arrested; and similar foolishness would certainly have been possible in October. And yet . . . "I can see why Shanker struck the first two times," said one of the most important (Negro) figures in the Ocean Hill unit. "Though you wouldn't expect it, because I'm out here and I'm loyal to this experiment and to these people, I even sympathize with him. But that third strike was just a horror."

Confusion of this sort is never necessary, but in this instance one must grant extenuating circumstance in the extraordinary presence of Rhody McCoy. For six months McCoy kept saying substantially different things to different people. He was against the original confrontation, but helped set it up; while appearing to favor arbitration of the dispute, he opposed even the Kheel recommendations at meetings of the governing board; throughout the summer he was discussing future joint ventures with Shanker while urging the community to continue its total intransigence to the return of Shanker's people; maintaining his image of professionalism and exclusive interest in education, he did not stop at the terrorism of the first Wednesday; during the strikes (and in the weeks following the final settlement) he was the source of any number of inflammatory statements and helped set up situations which would reveal what he called (correctly) the "degrading and humiliating" terms of the deal that had ended the strike—but each time one of his actions or statements made trouble, he could and did give a plausible explanation in terms of the demands upon him from "the community."

McCoy has an odd locution for his most disruptive statements: they are almost always put in the mouth of some anonymous other. Speaking about the radicalization of the governing board, for example, he said recently, "When a

107

mother sees her own kid failing, she thinks it's her fault or the kid's. When she sees a whole *class* of kids failing, then she begins to think the whole system is designed to keep black children down." The listener can come away from that statement believing either that McCoy himself thinks the school system is a deliberate conspiracy against Negroes or that he sympathizes with the violent but misdirected feelings of naïve women.

A foundation officer said the other day that he wished he could get some confidence that he knew the real McCoy. Members of the governing board would not be so clever about it, but sometimes they share the same view. McCoy keeps his pipe in his mouth, speaks slowly and not often, sometimes militantly, sometimes moderately, always intelligently. During Christmas week I challenged him with some of the inconsistencies detailed in this narrative, and with some others from the weeks after the end of the strike, and finally he said, "Everybody else seems to have a public posture and a private posture. Why shouldn't McCoy?" There is, I think, an answer to this, but I'm damned if I know what it is.

In the end, I suspect, what went wrong was that the second strike was too successful—it was actually *popular*. A member of the Board of Education says almost seriously that he believes Shanker called the third strike because he wants to be Mayor—and that if he ran he would win. The enormous turnouts at the teachers' rallies—five and ten times the size of the crowds that the followers of Ocean Hill could muster—ultimately persuaded the UFT that it could in effect refuse to deal with the elected Mayor of the city, and that it could dictate public policy on the continuance or abandonment of the Ocean Hill experiment. The strike revealed a shocking quantity of racist sentiment in the city, and among more teachers than one would have expected, especially given the leadership the teachers had chosen for themselves.

108

For Al Shanker was the leading integrationist in the New York labor movement. He marched in Selma, served on the steering committee of the Conference for Quality Integrated Education, and led the union's executive committee to a 30–2 endorsement of Mayor Lindsay's civilian review board to hear charges against the police. Not long before Ocean Hill blew up, Shanker proposed a civilian review board to deal with complaints against teachers from parents who found the existing disciplinary structure unresponsive to their anger.

Teacher lunchrooms were better integrated than any others I have ever seen, and Negroes probably felt more at home in the teachers' union than in any other white institution in the city. On the real issues that must be resolved in the city's schools, the UFT as an organization was by no means unsympathetic to the Negro side of the dispute.

But there were no real issues in the strikes—just slogans. What is ultimately disgusting about the teacher strikes and the public officials who failed to prevent them is that words like "community control" mean no more in dealing with the complex of relationships between school administrators and parents than words like "quality education" mean in dealing with the inadequate teacher training and severe multiple deprivation which combine to produce so much wretched work in our slum schools. On words like these, people who knew no better created a confrontation that damaged, perhaps irrevocably, the economic, social and political future of the greatest city in the world. There is no measuring the harm that was done. There is no excusing the leadership cadre who permitted it to be done.

PART IV

THINKING ABOUT
THE THINKABLE

"Projects, as they were called, were put forward in
great numbers by hangers-on of the Court."
—C. V. WEDGWOOD, *Social Comedy*
in the Reign of Charles I

"Get away from that wheelbarrow—what the hell do
you know about machinery?"
—attributed to ELBERT HUBBARD
by EUGENE MANLOVE RHODES

THE ARGUMENT which sustained the drive to decentralize
the New York schools was an insistence on the need for "accountability." In the centralized structure there were, simply,
too many distant authority figures who could be blamed for
unpopular decisions, for failure to respond to requests by
the parents whose children were, presumably, the bene-
ficiaries of the enterprise. Too many people could say no to
any change in existing procedure—especially any change in-
volving the reallocation of money or personnel. And, of
course, the principal or district superintendent who did not
want to do something found it easier to blame "110 Living-
ston Street" than to explain (let alone justify) his refusals.
Decentralization would knock away the crutches, would require the local hierarchs to be leaders rather than bureau-
crats, would promote responsibility through increasing authority.

111

But the three "demonstration units" sponsored by Ford in 1967 were in fact structured to avoid accountability. In spring 1968 the president of the IS-201 parents association complained that it was harder to get answers to questions from the governing board of that complex than it had been to get responses of some sort from the Board of Education—and the presidents of the parents associations in the Two Bridges unit unanimously petitioned the Board of Education to discontinue the experiment in their schools. There can be no question that the great majority of parents in Ocean Hill would have opposed the use of their schools and their children for the confrontation launched so disastrously on May 7, 1968, if they had known what was going on. But the parents— indeed, the parent representatives on the governing boards— have had no way to find out what is going on. Rhody McCoy did not say to them that if you have a broken foot you might as well get a broken hand, too.

Nobody can spend any time out on Ocean Hill without acquiring great affection for, and even a kind of loyalty to, the earnest mothers on the governing board and the eager, helpful young people on McCoy's staff. Unavoidably, however, both the mothers and the youngsters are very ignorant. Everyone's opinions are formed by the information he receives, and in areas like Ocean Hill contact with normal sources of information is minimal. Those individuals who are routinely in touch with the influential outside world—a McCoy, a Father Powis, a Rev. Oliver—will be able to control almost all the information that is received and credited by a group poorly equipped to judge what they are told. Moreover—and here there are unique opportunities for mischief— the influential outside world, ignorant of life in the "ghetto," learns about the inner group and its needs and attitudes only through the same people who control the flow of more general information to "the community."

In the end, then, nobody is responsible for anything. A McCoy does not (almost cannot) tell his governing board all that he is doing or that is being done to or for him—and whatever he does that seems discreditable on the outside he can blame on his governing board or on "the community." In the context of today, the situation radicalizes itself and becomes destructive almost without conscious effort, because those on the outside most interested in the ghetto want to hear about murder plots and revolutionary movements (makes them go goose pimples all over), while the more organized fraction inside wants to believe in Establishment conspiracies designed to frustrate the hopes of poor people. But in any context "community control" of complex public services cannot be discussed intelligently as desirable or undesirable, because it is thoroughly impossible. The supposed controllers will be controlled by their staff, because their staff will be their almost exclusive source of information.

This slavery to the staff also occurred all over the country, some years back, in suburban school systems, where otherwise sober-minded (indeed, highly conservative) school board members became apologists for the worst sillinesses of progressive education through the worst years of its decadence, because the inside information which was the mark of their office came to them through doctrinaire proponents of progressivism. In the suburbs, however, a reasonably sophisticated and literate voting public has to be convinced at intervals of the wisdom of the school board's policies—and an aggressive if ignorant right wing is always in evidence to provoke challenges which must be met. Our experience with "community control," indeed, comes from the suburban school board elections the right wing has won, which were typically followed by purges of "Communist" books from the library, inquisitions of the social studies teachers, etc.

In the slums the only persistent sources of contrary information are on the left, because the right does not care what happens in slums ("When you've seen one," etc.). The parents have no resources for challenging: having voted unanimously that Rev. Oliver should not enter J-271 against the orders of the state trustee, the parent representatives on the governing board knew no way to let the outside world hear that they had done so. And in situations like Ocean Hill, these days, there is a terrorist-extortionist element, not unlike the old Mafia, which finds apparently political action a useful cover for its activities and can be recruited to the service of those who are (with the best will in the world, because they know they are right) controlling the supposed controllers.

Some sense of some of these difficulties lies behind the usual insistence on "training programs for board members" which accompanies all decentralization proposals and which presumably would give the newcomers access to outside information and to less parochial standards of judgment. But such programs are always part of the proposals for the projects and never part of the projects themselves, partly because they lack sex appeal for the administrators of the projects (whose real authority they would reduce) and partly because nobody has the vaguest notion how to design such an educational effort or how to carry it through. You have to know a hell of a lot before you can intelligently tell a superintendent of schools what to do. . . . What happens in real life is that the money set aside for the training program gets paid directly to the poor people on the board of the project, by the staff they are supposed to be controlling.

The error in all the existing school decentralization proposals, as Max Rubin has shrewdly pointed out, is that they talk about the powers, privileges and responsibilities of school boards, when in fact effective control of the schools over any period of time lodges in the professional staff. The important functions of a school board (apart from raising money, which

114

decentralized city districts won't do) are the hiring of a superintendent and the development of internal, unpublicized procedures to keep him honest by insisting on good answers to good questions. It is not the board which needs leeway in the hiring of principals and APs—it is the local superintendent, who alone can be held accountable for the performance of his staff. A board can profitably occupy time making its superintendent look good, but a superintendent becomes useless for any purpose if he is asked to make his board look good. The root evil in politicizing the schools, especially as Mayor Lindsay sought to do it, is that it places the superintendent in a position where his first job is negative: to avoid any possible trouble for his board (or for the Mayor).

Concentrating on the role of the superintendent in a decentralized system does, of course, give away much of the argument which has somehow taken over as the driving force for a new organization of the school system—the argument that people need to feel control over their destinies, and that our political structures must thus be realigned to assure maximum "participation" by "the community." Most of this strikes me as nonsense; people can gain protection of sorts by joining groups (like unions) which exist to protect them—but it is part of the human condition that nobody, not even a Jack Kennedy, ultimately controls his destiny. Anyway, rational grownups are not demanding a larger say in how the school system operates; they are demanding a better school system. In the real world, it is a very unusual (and probably underemployed) man who is more interested in process than in results. Clearly, the results are more likely to satisfy more people if those who control the process are responsive to the hopes and fears and needs of their clientele. But the work of translating these hopes and fears and needs into an operational language must be performed by leadership. The call

115

for "participation" reflects nothing more and nothing less than a dissatisfaction with existing leadership.

This dissatisfaction is, I think, legitimate, and I am prepared to argue, rather tentatively at present, that part of the solution lies in breaking down the units of decision into smaller pieces, geographically and by function, to permit visible leadership to wrestle with perceived problems. I know from personal experience on a local school board that much leadership potential within the Negro and Puerto Rican neighborhoods now goes unnoticed and thus unrewarded by the outside world. But the doctrine of participation does not produce recognition for such leadership; it produces faction, loud meetings, inaction and frustration. In practice, the purpose of the doctrine has been to give entree to academicians and foundation fellows and the eager "change agents" of the poverty program, who are easily forgiven because they mean so well and so clearly know not what they do. They bring money, which is in terribly short supply in the slums, and all they ask in return, like Sir Oswald Moseley in England thirty-five years ago, is Action.

Like the Lindsay appointees to the Board of Education, who did not know enough to see the end results of their insistence on reopening J-271 the Sunday night before the third strike, the advocates of Action are ill-equipped to predict the consequences of reaction. At the ludicrous extreme, they will, like Jason Epstein in the *New York Review of Books* in spring 1968, call on the Negro community to confront its white oppressors sternly with a choice between "capitulation" and "genocide." If the outcome should be genocide, *tant pis*—Epstein will still be a vice-president of Random House and can find other hobbies. As they say around the criminal courts, the lawyer always goes home. Like the criminal lawyer, the academician or the foundation officer has no continuing relation, no enforceable responsibility, to his clients.

116

His job is secure however many mistakes he makes, and if his advice gets his clients into even worse trouble, he just never sees them again.

That rootless, independently funded people make problems in the body politic is not news—New York has Hearst in its history as a splendid example. For the essence of political life (in *all* systems of government) is a web of personal relations and loyalties along the chain of the hierarchy. The first and most important duty of the political leader is to choose the leaders on the lower level, who must be able to represent the wishes of their people and to deliver the support of their units when required. Where the leader finds elected representatives in office, he must make them his people, for his own effective functioning and for theirs. Where he seeks to create new political institutions, he must see to it that their leaders are people with whom he can work, who can effectively distribute to their following the largess that the institution spreads. Barring crisis conditions, incidentally, no violent interventions are necessary to secure such results; local groups are only too willing to have leaders known to be friends of those higher up. And the hierarchy of relations means that there is always someone at each level who can indeed be held responsible, and if necessary controlled, through normal procedures.

This discussion may seem remote from Ocean Hill and the teachers' strikes, but in fact such political realities and a failure to understand them are at the heart of the story. Politically, the Ocean Hill unit was an excrescence: an alternative procedure for the performance of certain governmental tasks which were already being performed by other agencies. Outside the normal chain of responsibility, it could and did look for rewards from many sources—from the Mayor's Urban Task Force, from Ford, from Kenneth Clark's contacts in the Board of Regents, from the Board of Education—without establishing a fixed relationship with any. Under the circumstances, a measure of gambling behavior was almost inevitable, yet none of these agencies developed anything like a plan to control trouble in the area. Indeed, Ford (which had been willing to flex muscle to force both Ocean Hill and IS-201 to abandon Herman Ferguson) inferentially supported Ocean Hill in its disastrous course by confirming its third grant after the May fiasco. Not the least of the political questions left dangling at the end of the tragedy of the teachers' strikes is the best way to make tax-exempt foundations responsible for the consequences of their actions. For here, too, boards are at the mercy of partial information directed at them by their staffs.

On a higher level of generalization, our problems in education are merely a special case of the root problem of politics in a modern society: the control of professional performance. It is nonsense to believe that amateurs (gentlemen, scholars or black militants) can successfully operate the immensely complicated machinery of modern government. Yet the modern professional's commitment to his own machine—the court system for resolving disputes, hospital care for minor ailments, the self-contained classroom with basal readers—can produce ridiculous and indefensible cost-benefit ratios. Except for college teachers, professionals typically work hard, but the end value of their labors is reduced by their tendency to develop licensing procedures at entry rather than quality control in action. Because they are the masters of their own mysteries, the professionals must be given a large measure of self-direction, but they are after all part of a larger society which supports them, and when they ignore the needs and purposes of that society to serve their own shibboleths (as educators especially tend to do), they become parasites. The failure of public education to respond to societal demand is especially discouraging, because here there is a public in-

118

stitution—the school board—which presumably exercises some continuing authority.

Our schools suffer from failures of leadership and of technique. Ultimately, the justification for decentralization must be that it will promote the discovery of new leadership and stimulate (via competition among districts) the development of better techniques. We need such justification badly, by the way, because *theoretically* decentralization must be harmful to poorer and less well-educated districts. McCoy at one time seemed a fine example of the sort of leadership a centralized system unfairly kept down. Now, of course, the possible discovery of one, two, many McCoys, while a fascinating prospect, seems a little less clearly a boon to the city's children.

To McCoy and many of his colleagues all this commentary will be *Hamlet* without the Dane, because it ignores the race issue. Some readers will have spotted me as the fink I am from early on, because I use the word "Negro" rather than the word "black." But I have the feeling that most of the Negroes I know are uncomfortable about the word "black." It is the word Southern slaveowners applied to their slaves, and South African and Rhodesian rulers still apply to their African subjects. The word is to some extent negative in every language I know, and must continue to be so, because the grave is black and the heavens are bright and the preference for day over night is bred in the bones of the human species. Think of all the pleasant connotations of the word "colored" by contrast with the connotations of the word "black." It is even inaccurate as a description. And by forcing the contrast black/white it insists on a classic dichotomy which is in large part nonsense now and must become total nonsense in the future.

Education is a cultural and not a racial question. No ethnic group has managed as many as three generations in this country without becoming Americanized beyond the recognition of the former home folks, and it is now at least six and seven generations beyond the arrival of the ancestors of American Negroes, three full generations since Emancipation. Seen from outside, the story has been absorbed; there is no separate Negro history. The failure to teach Negro history is really a special case of the general failure to teach working-class history. The neglect of the writings of James Weldon Johnson is just as shocking in white classrooms as in Negro classrooms, for any study of American literature should have an input from one of the most stylish writers and interesting minds of the first third of this century.

Though there is, of course, a respectable tradition of Negro separatism—casting down one's bucket where one is, as Booker T. Washington put it—the effort to impose an African culture on the modern American Negro is as fake (and as funny) as teaching Gaelic to the kids of Irish cops. In terms of day-to-day schoolwork, I suspect there are values in teaching Swahili rather than French to Negro children who want Swahili (teachers will expect them to do well in Swahili, which is a reasonable fraction of the battle; and never mind the fact that Swahili is a slave trader's argot from a part of East Africa which is farther from the point of origin of American Negroes than Moscow is from London). But Negro separatism in my observation of it has invariably been a gesture not of pride but of despair. It is like a high protective tariff which seeks to nurture infant industries; and like the high tariff it leads to shoddy goods, inefficiency and unjust enrichment of a powerful few.

Certainly there is no evidence whatever for the argument that Negro students do better in school when their teachers and administrators are Negro. The students who are in the worst shape in all the Northern cities are those who came from the segregated school systems of the South, where all

120

their teachers and principals were Negro. That's different, say the militants, because *those* were subservient Negroes. But there are several low-income Negro suburbs in New York and New Jersey, where Negro administrators have been running almost all-Negro school districts with Negro staffs, and the results are simply abysmal.

Of course there should be more Negro teachers and administrators in the New York schools, just as there should be more Negro advertising men and Wall Street brokers and lawyers and doctors. And of course professional entry standards which do not relate to performance on the job—as the New York City elementary principals' competitive exam does not—should not be permitted to keep capable Negroes out of positions they could fill. But the poor performance of Negro children in our schools is an American problem, not a Negro problem. Its solution must command American resources if only because Negro resources are nowhere near great enough to deal with it. And the value system by which one judges what is done in these schools must be no different from that which would be applied to other American schools. Excusing bigotry or terrorism or fraud in Negro life because of "three hundred years of oppression" is discrimination directly comparable to police failure to prosecute assaults or gambling or narcotics in the slums; whatever the revolutionary or empathic jargon in which such double standards are expressed, what is really being said is that you can't expect any better from these people. It is equally shocking that some reputable Negro leadership has been willing to ask such indulgences and that sophisticated political and academic leadership has been willing to grant them.

In one of the least intelligent public comments on the school crisis of fall 1968, the New York Urban Coalition published an ad proclaiming that what's good enough for Scarsdale is good enough for Ocean Hill. In fact, of course,

121

the quality of the Scarsdale school system (which I must say I find overadvertised) depends from the high educational level and even higher levels of ambition of the parent community; if you transported it bodily to Ocean Hill, the results, educationally and politically, would be catastrophic. The argument one can intelligently make is that what's *not* good enough for Scarsdale is not good enough for Ocean Hill. And race is no excuse.

Nevertheless, though the proximate causes of the teachers' strikes were the unwillingness and inability of official leadership to handle a predictable and manageable problem, these problems will eventually cease to be manageable unless the schools find ways to educate to higher levels of performance a higher proportion of children like those who live in Ocean Hill. It is vicious behavior to exploit for political purposes people's fears for their children's future, and no set of attitudes is more surely counterproductive than the politics of despair. But it is the promise—and the genius—of America that generations do not reproduce themselves as they were before, and that promise must be kept.

This said, it remains important to remember that Melville's Confidence Man was also part of the American genius; and that everybody who's talking about Heaven ain't going there. An ill-marked and undefended border separates meaning well from meaning nothing at all. In a society which believes fundamentally that government rests on documents, that border is quickly crossed. We are on the wrong side of it now in New York, and somehow we must scramble back.

About the Author

Martin Prager Mayer was born in New York in 1928; both his parents are lawyers. He was graduated in 1947 from Harvard, where he majored in economics and also studied philosophy and music.

Mr. Mayer is uniquely qualified to write this report on the New York teachers' strike. From 1961 to 1965 he was a member of the Panel on Educational Research and Development in the Executive Office of the President, and from 1962 to 1967 he was chairman of a New York City local school board. In 1962 he published one of the first articles making the case for decentralization. He is the author of *The Schools,* a report on American education based on visits to over one hundred schools in the United States, and of *Where, When and Why* (titled *Social Studies in American Schools* in its paperback edition), a report made to the American Council of Learned Societies and the Carnegie Corporation. His report on international secondary education was published in 1968 by the Twentieth Century Fund, under the title *Diploma.*

He has also written two novels and three other reportorial studies: *Wall Street: Men and Money; Madison Avenue, U.S.A.;* and *The Lawyers.* He is, as well, the author of a biography, *Emory Buckner,* published in 1968 under the auspices of the William Nelson Cromwell Foundation, and of *All You Know Is Facts*, a collection of his magazine articles, published in 1969. His articles on education, business, television, music, law, and other subjects have appeared in *Esquire, Harper's, Saturday Evening Post, Fortune, TV Guide, Better Homes & Gardens, Life, The New York Times Magazine, Horizon, Musical America*, and *Commentary*, among others.

Mr. Mayer serves in various advisory or trustee roles for the University of Illinois Arithmetic Project, *Opera News*, the New York Pro Musica, and the United Nations International School. He is married to the writer and scholar Ellen Moers. They have two sons, Thomas and James.

Design by Sidney Feinberg
Set in Linotype Caledonia
Composed, printed and bound by American Book–Stratford Press, Inc.
HARPER & ROW, PUBLISHERS, INCORPORATED